IT'S IN OUR NATURE

Edited by

James Feeke

First published in Great Britain in 2003 by
POETRY NOW
Remus House,
Coltsfoot Drive,
Peterborough, PE2 9JX
Telephone (01733) 898101
Fax (01733) 313524

All Rights Reserved

Copyright Contributors 2003

HB ISBN 1 84460 956 1
SB ISBN 1 84460 957 X

FOREWORD

Although we are a nation of poets we are accused of not reading poetry, or buying poetry books. After many years of listening to the incessant gripes of poetry publishers, I can only assume that the books they publish, in general, are books that most people do not want to read.

Poetry should not be obscure, introverted, and as cryptic as a crossword puzzle: it is the poet's duty to reach out and embrace the world.

The world owes the poet nothing and we should not be expected to dig and delve into a rambling discourse searching for some inner meaning.

The reason we write poetry (and almost all of us do) is because we want to communicate: an ideal; an idea; or a specific feeling. Poetry is as essential in communication, as a letter; a radio; a telephone, and the main criterion for selecting the poems in this anthology is very simple: they communicate.

CONTENTS

Awakening	Di Bagshawe	1
When I Hear That Sound	Milly Hatcher	2
Beholding Spring	Maureen Newman	3
Dark Spring	Terry O'Reilly	4
Untitled	Ray Smart	5
Early Spring Morning	R Law	6
Spring Has Come	Sarah Nicholson	7
March	June Worsell	8
Broadwater In Spring	Uvedale Tristram	9
Spring	Pamela Carder	10
Three Faces Of Spring	Philip Worth	11
I Rescue Daffodils	Valerie Perring	12
The Silent Monarch	Ted Pryor	13
Spring's Celebration	Joanna Maria John	14
Spring	Joy Morton	15
Spring	Shirley Wasylyk	16
Spring Fever	Sue Mackenzie	17
Ectopia	Lucy Crispin	18
Spring On Romney Marsh	Brenda Lismer	19
It Must Be Spring	Catherine Torode	20
Spring	Kirsty Virgo	21
Spring Is Here	June Melbourn	22
Springtime Madness	Lilian Owen	23
Nature's Gifts	Claudia Thompson	24
The Arrival Of Spring	Joe Loxton	25
Seasons	Dorothy Buyers	26
Symptoms Of Spring	Felicity M Greenfields	27
Spring	Nicola Barnes	28
Springtime	Steven Gunning	29
April	Angela Pritchard	30
Spring Equinox	Anita Richards	31
The Prince Of Spring	Dorothy Chadwick	32
Haiku	Colette Thomson	33
Spring Love	Daniela Morbin	34
Awaken	Alice Hemming	35
Snowdrops	Eileen Burgess	36

Title	Author	Page
Homeless	Henry Disney	37
Melody Of Spring	Ann G Wallace	38
Spring Wood	Robert D Shooter	39
B-r-r-r-r-r-r!	Edward L Smith & Carmen M Pursifull	40
Perfect Start	Chris Silvester	41
The First Snowdrop	Suie Nettle	42
Change	B R Walker	43
Spring Song	Norrie Ferguson	44
Come Spring	John Brackenbury	45
The Red Lion, Avebury	Indy Clark	46
Spring	Jacqueline Hartnett	47
There's A Glory In The Springtime	Peter Spurgin	48
So Great To Behold	E Marcia Higgins	49
The Joys Of Spring	Theresa Griffiths	50
Right On Time	Jo Hodson	51
Let Nature Sing	Olliver Charles	52
Spring	Beryl Sylvia Rusmanis	53
Bluebells - The Heralds Of Spring	Constance Vera Dewdney	54
Early Morning Magic	Paula J Holt	55
Woodland In Winter	David A Garside	56
Spring To Summer	David Rosser	57
Nature's Revenge	Gary J Finlay	58
Seasonally Affective Disorder	Diane Burrow	59
The Bells That Toll On A Summer's Day	Anne Veronica Tisley	60
The Golden Orb	Roma Davis	61
An Ancient Churchyard In Spring (Caverswall)	John Pegg	62
Spring Lambs	Carolyn Smith	63
Rainfall	Emily McLeod	64
Spring Promise	Phillipa Grundy	65
The Breath Of Spring	Josephine Thomas	66
The Walk	Sabina Kelly	67
The Sermon Of Spring	David Bridgewater	68
Winter's Sleep	Jefferson Hammond	69
Overhead Buzzing Cables	Neville Anthony	70

Title	Author	Page
April Is The Cruellest Month	Michael A Fenton	71
Old Winter's Death!	Laraine Smith	72
Gardener's Joy	Kathleen Gilboy	73
Spring . . . A New Beginning	Arthur Pickles	74
Spring Is In The Air	Coleen Bradshaw	75
Spring	Rowena Haley	76
Stony Path	Mary Guckian	77
April	Jean Atkinson	78
Spring 1940	Jack Major	79
The Breath Of Spring	Marisa Greenaway	80
Stover Nature Park	Margaret Gurney	81
Mud	Liz Osmond	82
The Robin	Rose-Marie Bonnevier	83
Spring Is In The Air	Muriel Berry	84
Spring Symphony	Carole Harradence	85
The Stirring Of Spring	Eira Chapman	86
March Winds	Kerri Fordham	88
Autumn Fever	Samina Amjad	89
Green-Laced Oasis	Roger Thornton	90
Sunflower	Ruby Debnam	91
Hills	Janet Eirwen Smith	92
Wonders Of The Deep	A Higham	93
Paintings In The Clouds	Doreen Petherick Cox	94
Summer Storm	Ann Hathaway	95
Integrity	Doug Ramsay	96
Spectres Vapid	C J Bayless	98
Listen And Look!	Dorothy J White	99
For Eyes That Don't See	Susan E Roffey	100
Beside The Shore	Valerie L Warsop	101
Morning Glory	Nicky Ridsdale	102
Country Walks	Lachlan Taylor	103
Tulipomania	Val Plant	104
The Eden Project	Lorna June Burdon	106
Trees	Irene Siviour	107
Natural Break	James Thomson	108
Nature's Voices	Margaret B Baguley	110
Cavern Of Weeds . . . The Pike	Viv Lionel Borer	111
Where Will It End?	Aline McInnes Ross	112

World Of Conflict	Finnan Boyle	113
The World	Sheun Oshinbolu	114
The Pride And The Passion	R N Taber	115
Coastline	Paul Kelly	116
Autumnal	Carole A Cleverdon	117
See Of Array	Hugh Campbell	118
Aesthetic Setting	Noel Thaddeus Lawler	119
Where I Love To Be	Carol Ann Darling	120
Flowers In The Springtime	Janet Cavill	121
Feeling My Senses	Christine Taylor	122
Nature's Bounty	D Parry	123
Freedom	Irene Grahame	124
The Ridgeway	J M Gardener	125
The Crocus	Harry Lyons	126
Stars	I Mackenzie	127
Autumn	Marc Shemmans	128
Soaring High	Agnes Neeson	129
Clematis	Pat Heppel	130
The Windylehoo!	Micaela Beckett	131
Roses	Joan Prentice	132
Full Moon Over Cardiff Bay	Guy Fletcher	133
Mother Earth	Patricia Gray	134
Wild Daffodils	Norma Rudge	135
The River	Diana Price	136
The Spirit Of Life	Margaret H Mustoe	137
The Enchanting Cranbourne Chase	Sammy Davis	138
The Rocks	Philip Allen	139
The Daisies Sung	Victoria Garbutt	140
Four Seasons	M M Graham	141
The Rose	Brian Mcdonagh	142
Snowflake	Norman Bissett	143
Spring In Somerset	Monica Redhead	144
Springtime In Cairo	Suzanna Wilson	145
The Autumn Of Life	Margaret Nixon	146
Seasoned Gratitude	Clive Cornwall	147
The Hunter	Robert Allen	148
Rainy Days	Rosalia Campbell Orr	149

Nature's Disappearing	Mary Pauline Winter	150
Mother Earth	L E Marchment	151
The Black Hole	John Chambers	152
Was That A Forecast?	Kathleen Townsley	154

AWAKENING

When spring's warm days call 'Come alive!'
And twitch the counterpane of Earth,
Send sun to wake the slumbering hive,
Frissons of energy for new birth.
Snowdrops and crocus test the air,
Daffodils raise a trumpet blast,
Decorous blossoms peep from branches bare,
Earth's colours have returned at last.
Birds in a frenzy to mate
Bicker until their choice is bound,
Nest confined, alert they wait,
Protecting from the dangers round.
Young born within the winter's cell
Intoxicated by freedom found,
With easier living grow and swell,
Delighted explore the world around.
Gaunt trees dress again in leaves,
Vie to wear the brightest shade.
Pollen from catkins the bee retrieves
Ferrying so new plants are made.
Dead twigs burst into bud,
Hidden safe encased from cold
Grass mats over winter's mud,
Kingcups rim the ponds with gold.
All the tender burgeoning life
Pray spring's siren call is true
And frost's vicious killing knife
Is sheathed, until the growing's through.

Di Bagshawe

WHEN I HEAR THAT SOUND

When I hear that sound, I know its' spring -
From every tree their voices ring.
Birds, bursting their throats as if in praise,
With thrushes repeating each lilting phrase.

The birds sing sweetly, then give an encore.
The world has become to its liking once more.
Bubbly notes rising, the lark flies up high,
Then slowly fades as it reaches the sky.

Then, in full-throated melody the blackbirds sing,
With Heavenly notes to welcome spring.
The warm sunshine does its best
And the birds are busy building their nests.

And when the baby robins sing
You know for sure it is the spring.
Now winter has gone, spring gives new birth
To all the living things on Earth.

Milly Hatcher

BEHOLDING SPRING

I went for a bus ride and what did I see?
The greens of the fields, the buds on the tree.
The deep brown of new ploughed earth,
The sheep heavy with young ready to give birth.
The birds chasing and flirting in love's ritual sweet,
Others make nests all coy and neat.
The bright sunshine yellow of the trumpeted daffodil,
Young foals nuzzling their mums gave me a thrill.
As I sat on that bus on that day in early spring,
We passed through a village as a church bell did ring.
I saw a young man gaze at his new wife, oh to witness such love.
Yes, my dear friends, love, for that's what spring is all about,
God's love to mankind as He shows us His care as the fields
and gardens wake up to new life with a shout.
Ready and willing to produce good fare, corn, wheat and barley are
but a few,
Potatoes, peas and beans all growing anew.
As God paints the files with a cacophony of colour,
I ride on and evening comes, the clouds form a blanket and everything
looks duller.
Then just as you think everything's gone to sleep, out from behind
a cloud the sun takes a peep.
At last the bus arrives back in town leaving the countryside dressed
in her nightgown.
Spring, my dear friends is such a delight, but till the morrow
I must say,
God bless and goodnight ...

Maureen Newman

DARK SPRING

Spring, but no fresh shoots of hope for me.
No rising spirits in the new season's dawn.
No rebirth, no flowering anew.

Since your passing,
In my soul, only the dark of a perpetual winter's night.

But with memories come the bliss of knowing you.
And in dreaming, glimpse again the bright springs
That we once shared.

Terry O'Reilly

UNTITLED

Small bird singing in the willow tree.
Clouds like cotton, moving easily.
Phoebus rising and increasingly
Warming winter-hardened ground.

Dark days dying, there's a sense of joy,
Spring arriving brings a symphony
Of hope returning to the cold damp earth,
As she spreads her happiness around.

Peace prevailing in the angry heart.
Love remaining as the major part
Of life with meaning, for the world is good
With warmth and sunlight in the mind.

Ray Smart

EARLY SPRING MORNING

The leaves of green on grey of fen in
morning mists ghostly glow.
As morning chorus fills the air of
breezes through lank grass you go.
Trickling water under well-trodden foot
bridge and ducks, chasing and quacking
to and fro in rippled wake.
The river mist shimmers lightly over the water
and green grass shines through.
Walking along the towpath the boathouses appear
through hazy clouds disconnected from the shore.
In the distance the road bridge heralds the start of
the commuter's day, a mechanical road sweeper brushes
whirring motor revving glides by and then rushes off,
leaving cool morning mist to settle on road again.

R Law

SPRING HAS COME

A heron stands by the edge of the pond
Silent, motionless, patiently waiting
He has been there since two hours or beyond
For the surface of the water breaking
Beneath the water the female frog watches
With bulging eyes the dagger sharp beak
Ready poised to pluck her from the batches
Of newly laid eggs exhausted and weak
I clap my hands and shout
The heron rises slowly from the ground
The frog quickly turns about
And disappears below the lily pads without a sound
Suddenly from among the forsythia's yellow blooms
The beautiful song of a robin fills the air
His heart is joyful, his breast bright red plumes
'Tis spring he has found a mate, they have a nest to prepare
A blackbird scrapes beneath the green budded shrubs
Kicking winter's dead leaves pecking the earth
Searching intensely for fresh grubs
Brought to the surface by the sun's warmth
Then I notice the most wonderful sight of all
Snowdrops, crocuses and daffodils bedded together
Like a luxurious carpet wall to wall
All heralding another season regardless of the weather
Life suddenly to me seems brighter
I return indoors and begin to softly hum
The dark clouds above me have become lighter
A little prayer of thanks . . . spring has come

Sarah Nicholson

MARCH

Unleashed the energy of life,
The power surge of early spring,
Woodlands rejoice in fluting song,
Music from every feathered wing.

Warbler polishes his repertoire,
Shyly preferring to be unseen,
Amid the confusion of budding twigs
And hawthorns flush of timbered green.

Violets hug the cool and shade,
In quiet beauty and modest pose,
Humble and often overlooked,
Perfumed to rival any rose.

Primroses line the sunny banks,
Drinking in the warming rays,
Bathed in nature's soothing light,
Their gift of life repays.

Beside the busy country road
Tiny lilac buds unlock,
Dancing in the morning air,
Blooms the pastel lady smock.

Wary is this month of March,
To waver winter's grip is folly,
For though the world looks fine today,
There's still a berry on the holly.

June Worsell

BROADWATER IN SPRING

The dying sun at close of day
Has cast a gleam upon the lake.
The bare branched trees are mirrored there
In sunset glow upon the waterway
And in the twilight now the night birds wake
And beauty thrusts away all human fear.

The darkling lake at start of night
Still holds the image of the trees,
Bare branched still in burgeoned spring
And gentle ripples stir the light
That dances in the evening breeze
To speed the heron's homeward wing.

The mile of lake through Oatlands field
Still trembles with half forgotten shame -
Half mad Henry and his discarded wives
Where love and life to lust and terror yields -
Purest Catherine and her falsely plotted blame -
The mindless evil that the water screens.

Uvedale Tristram

SPRING

Feel the stirrings in the hedgerow,
New lambs, frisking in the field,
Snowdrops white as fallen snow,
Soon will winter slowly yield
To spring.

Espy the yellow primrose,
As its face turns to the sun
Golden catkins, like candles hang
Soon will winter's frost be gone,
It's spring.

Greet Mother Nature's marvels
As birdsong trills on high,
Winter has shed her sombre cloak,
Embrace the golden canopy
Of spring.

Pamela Carder

THREE FACES OF SPRING

Spring is 'Old Tyme Music Hall'
With spotlight on,
Conductor bowing, roll of drums
And 'Overture Beginners Please';
Then 'Curtain Up' and MC waving arms
And calling for each act in turn -
The dancing, laughing, singing, naughty acts
That crowd through summer's bill.

Spring is when the world gets back its voice
Which falters, fades, grows dumb at the year's end,
When birds no longer sing
And water, turned to ice, forgoes its lapping,
And leaves, long gone, have ceased their whispering
And men, for warmth, of words are sparing.
Now there's talk, proclaiming
All the things that fill the lengthening days.

Spring is the kindly face of God
In easing us towards our end;
His time of giving
Every year a little less
Than earlier winter's taking.
So the deficits pile up
Like gently falling snow
Not noticed till the world is white.

Philip Worth

I Rescue Daffodils

Defeated by a storm, or someone's boot,
I find them wounded, face-first in the grass,
Not dead but slowly running out of life
Unless they find a stretcher-bearer fast.

From public places, churchyards and our own
Communal garden where the cat is king,
I raise the fallen blooms and bring them home.
Thinking myself protective, sheltering,

I mark the random kindness of the Lord
Who made them delicate to touch the heart.
Would I get muddy for a dandelion
Or bow the knee before a thistle plant?

Some offer nuts to squirrels, others feed
Bread to the glossy mallards on the lake.
Each to his kind of giving. As for me,
I rescue daffodils, for my own sake.

Valerie Perring

THE SILENT MONARCH
(On the birth of a Monarch butterfly in my garden)

Patiently you held onto an unfurled leaf,
under which your broken chrysalis forlornly swayed.
Four long weeks we waited for
the gift of your miracle transformation.

As we slumbered deep, you struggled long
to break free from your cradle-like shelter,
and emerged exhausted to be showered
and dried by the first rays of a bright dawn.

Then - after two circles of the clock - hesitantly,
you clapped together your dazzle-coated wings
and, with a silent purpose, set sail on a gentle
breeze like an autumn leaf - to be seen no more.

Ted Pryor

SPRING'S CELEBRATION

In an earthen bed in a border grow the gladiolus,
petals red, pink or white,
the colour of the clouds in the blue skies
roses white, yellow, pink, red and maroon
all dancing in the afternoon,
tulips have sturdy stems they stand upright,
petals yellow, pink, red, purple and white,
daffodil petals have a little frilly trim,
their stems are sturdy and slim
geraniums red, pink and white
such a delight,
fuchsias are pink and plum,
they flower one by one,
leaves are sprouting,
showers fall like a fountain,
marigold petals are like the sun's rays,
they enjoy the warm sunny days
the cornflower is deep blue like the seas,
gently swaying in the cool breeze,
lavender grows like wheat, scented sweet,
the bumblebee is ever so busy,
he collects nectar from roses,
honeysuckle candytuft and the busy lizzy
oh how pretty they are all made
they close their petals in the evening's glade,
forget-me-nots are the colour of the blue skies,
they open their petals in the early morning sunrise,
they all grow in spring's celebration,
not forgetting the single and double
red, yellow, pink and white carnation.

Joanna Maria John

SPRING

As Britain turns to face the sun
Days extending, warmth absorbing
Promise-filled rebirth recurs
In God's dependency.

Sunshine and showers slake
The esurient Earth,
Decorating the heart-land
In technicolour dream-blossoms.
And in the ever-greening fields,
Life-ready lambs spring forth to play
Subliminal symbols
Of this annual cycle of wonder.

Joy Morton

SPRING

Spring has arrived with the bulbs all a peeping,
Dare we grow on? Have the frost finished reaping?
The shrubs and the trees, the bushes and plants,
All show new life if we just care to glance.
The birds in the garden are prancing and playing,
The summer is coming they seem to be saying.
The cold winter winds that ranted and raved,
The snow and the ice that we all had to brave.
Their time in the seasons is part of the past,
So now with the spring let's look forward at last.

Shirley Wasylyk

SPRING FEVER

Is it possible that spring is round the corner,
Though the winter frosts lie heavy on the ground?
For in a sheltered corner of my garden,
Dainty snowdrops dancing in the breeze I've found.
The billing and the cooing from our songbirds,
Signifies that love is in the air
And if you were to rise before the cock crows,
The awakening of the day, with God you'd share.
Can you feel that overwhelming magic moment,
As the watery shafts of sunlight kiss the earth,
Rejuvenating buds that once lay dormant,
Heralding the wonder of new birth?
Springtime holds a fairytale enchantment.
It heightens senses, sets the spirit free.
A season overflowing with charisma,
That activates the dream machine in me.
So glad farewells to bitter winds and grey skies,
As the wheels of time roll onwards down the track,
Inspiring 'Mother Nature' in her wisdom
To bring about a 'spring fever' attack.

Sue Mackenzie

ECTOPIA

There seems no place for sorrow in spring,
when fresh life frills branches, and birds
charm their mates across the brightening air.

Tulips, fat-leaved, are shouldering their way
up through the waking earth, more full
of bluster than the cautious snowdrops;

crocus-clumps are shouting to the sun
as it limbers up after winter's rest, and daffodils
are egg-yolk brazen, or egg-white delicate,

as they bob and ring in the nudging breeze.
There seems no place for loss, when so much
is given: no place for stasis, when the world

is moving on; and so I wear my grief in silence,
well-wrapped and buried like the seeds I trust
to the spring-warmed earth - the sand-grain

in the oyster, where acceptance works irritation
into iridescence, and new beauty may be born
of trouble, given time, oh, given time.

Lucy Crispin

SPRING ON ROMNEY MARSH

This is where spring begins
Year after year,
Below the ridge
Where the wind is stilled
And the sun is warm on the marshland.
Where ancient stones
Stand yet against the years,
Breathing of Roman times
And ewes in lamb graze comfortably,
Chewing the cud and waiting their time.

Here I am released from winter's bonds,
And the self-doubt of darker days,
To be renewed at earth's awakening
And glad to be in on it.

Brenda Lismer

IT MUST BE SPRING

Pink and white blossoms to be seen on the trees,
petals blown to the ground by the warm gentle breeze,

birds singing, and shaking their wings,
there comes to my mind just one thing,
        It must be spring.

The soil left behind, the flowers peep through,
Daffodils, tulips and hyacinths too,

Wild daisies, and dandelions and crocuses as well,
and more of which the names I can't tell.

The lark in the sky, the frogs croaking by,
there comes to my mind just one thing,
        It must be spring.

The evenings growing longer and lighter also,
the sun in the sky beginning to glow,

heavy winter clothes cast aside,
young men looking for a sweet bride,

there comes to mind just one thing,
        It must be spring.

Catherine Torode

SPRING

Spring is here,
it's time for cheer;
we're drinking wine;
we're guzzling beer.

    Flowers growing,
    mowers mowing,
    trees bowing,
    farmers hoeing.

Spring is here,
it's the time of year;
we're having fun;
the sky is clear.

    Flowers growing,
    mowers mowing,
    trees bowing,
    farmers hoeing.

Spring has gone;
we're back at step one,
but do not fear;
as summer is here!

Kirsty Virgo (10)

SPRING IS HERE

The longer days are here at last,
Still light at half past four,
It's feeling warmer, so celebrate,
Spring is knocking at the door.

The garden, for a long time drab,
Now colour is coming through,
Crocuses, primroses, daffodils,
Pansies, in all shades of blue.

Many birds are visiting
The table for the bread,
It's time to grease the lawnmower
Lying dormant in the shed.

The sun is trying hard to shine,
The plants are sprouting, buds are seen,
The trees, so long brown and bare,
They are starting to turn green.

The newborn lambs frolic in the fields,
Such joy to us they bring,
The catkins on the woodland walks,
So welcoming is spring!

June Melbourn

SPRINGTIME MADNESS

An English spring aglow with daffodils,
while a war erupts in the desert sand.
From the top bough of a tree a bird trills,
so find it difficult to understand
why the world cannot be a peaceful place,
all nations agreeing, dealing in trade,
regardless of colour, culture or race
where children can play, unharmed, unafraid.
Whilst the spring evolves in all its glory,
with trees bursting forth into tender green
the Middle East, a different story
ugly face of war shown on TV screen.
Planes bombing, tanks in ominous convoy
chaos all around, has the world gone mad?
Instead of gladness, so hard to enjoy
springtime sunshine, I find it very sad.

Lilian Owen

NATURE'S GIFTS

Golden sun and blustery showers,
Daffodils, tulips and primrose flowers,
Catkins, buds and blossom on trees,
Branches swaying in the breeze.
Beauty in a world that's new,
Spring is here, winter is through.

Newborn lambs in fields of green,
Boxing hares scattered between,
Nests with mother birds on eggs,
Ponds with tadpoles growing legs.
Wonder in a world that's new,
Spring is here, winter is through.

Waking hedgehogs looking for food,
Hens and ducks parading their brood,
Seedlings drinking drops of rain,
Cuckoos come to sing again.
Enchantment in a world that's new,
Spring is here, winter is through.

Expanding cities, workload powers,
Technology controlling leisure hours.
We need to pause and look around,
To note each seasonal sight and sound.
For, sadly, I feel we are less aware,
Of nature's gifts everywhere.

Claudia Thompson

THE ARRIVAL OF SPRING

Water, snow and ice,
Underneath, a curtain of green,
In pursuit of change,
Soon the unquiet spirit will confront the world,
With the arrival of spring,
There will be new life for old cemeteries,
Plants for show,
Like manna from Heaven,
From the wild,
Magic sanctuaries,
For natural partnerships,
The secret reeds will take bold steps,
To cover the crake's last stand,
The banshee will examine his way of being,
Whilst behind the lines,
In the quiet of a loving eye,
The kingfisher will renew his love affair with nature.

Joe Loxton

SEASONS

Spring was only a moment -
A moment of petals from a cherry tree,
A white enchantment drifting to Earth,
To the dark soil that holds
The treasure of former springs, fragmented,
The lost beauty of withered primroses
And crocus, and the beauty of summer
Sealed in the roots of the rose.

Summer passed swiftly as a day -
A moment of roses seen from a train,
Disappearing; a passenger seen
Across the aisle; a moment of desire
As eyes meet, without words, while the train
Hurtles on towards separate stations,
Leaving only a memory to grow
In silence in the mind.

Dorothy Buyers

SYMPTOMS OF SPRING

The sun has shone today,
it made me feel so good.
Although in saying that,
the trees still have no buds.

The birds are visible to see;
the blue tit sings its song,
he sounds, for all the world;
like a rusty hacksaw blade.

The robin has a sweeter voice,
its blood red chest displayed.
Informing me and all around,
spring's not so far away.

Then of course the butterflies,
rest, on garden mint and bay.
They seem for all the world to tell,
spring's just about to come.

Crocuses, daffodils and snowdrops
have popped their heads up too.
As if to reassure us,
spring really has arrived.

But why, I wonder are the buds,
still absent form the trees?
Has spring really come, I ponder,
or just fooled us, once, again?

Felicity M Greenfields

SPRING

The daffodil
Fills
The
Garden.
The first
Clump
Seen
In
Spring
Along
The
Roadside
Gardenwise.

Nicola Barnes

SPRINGTIME

One morning the dew awoke
and knew that spring had arrived at last

Through winter's bitter, dark embrace
some life still flickered behind our eyes

And the spring unfolded in our open hands
and pulsed into the fresh new land

And the gardens of the world were strewn
with garlands of a life renewed

So alike our spring in Eden
before the serpent spread its lies

So strange that we could not remember
despite all the seasons of our restless lives

That faith is precious as the springtime
and doubt is hidden in disguise

So spring - guide us forward on our journey!
give us grace and recompense

For we are like this changing landscape
longing so for innocence!

Steven Gunning

APRIL

Welcome to April,
A month full of contrasts,
Showers providing natural spring-cleaning
Wash off winter's grime.
Warm sunny days deceive,
Giving us snapshots of future summer bliss.

Angela Pritchard

SPRING EQUINOX

There's bread and cheese in the hedgerows,
the sweetest of scent fills the air.
There's a gangbang on the duck pond,
Spring Equinox is here.

There's a full moon sailing the Heavens,
through a thousand sparkling stars.
But Mars flashes beyond the horizon,
heralding battle scars.

For Tornadoes have circled and flown,
and our Fleet has left our shores.
And our Troops serve in the desert,
fighting some bloody war.

Anita Richards

THE PRINCE OF SPRING

Now the winter winds have ceased,
The snowstorms are no more.
Birds have returned from lands afar,
And frozen lakes have thawed.
See the sun a little warmer,
Shine across the glistening sea,
Spring just like a handsome prince,
Adorned in snowdrops, suddenly appears.
We all sing praises to the Heavens,
Hearts feel so joyous, spirits light.
Eastertime when He died upon the cross,
To rid the world of evil, wickedness and sin,
And give us all a happy life.
Children gather springtime flowers,
They all laugh and dance and sing,
Crocus, iris, daffodils,
All the beautiful blossoms to make a perfect garland,
For the prince of spring.

Dorothy Chadwick

HAIKU

Once upon a dream
I went to a wonderland
Where love never fades

Colette Thomson

SPRING LOVE
(Dedicated to my mum and Sally)

A feeling of spring love is wonderful
Mother and friends all around
The season gives way to burst of joy
And colours in bright confusion.

The harmony of true loves
And the happiness mother and friends bring
Is like a crocus budding in the sunlight
Yellow, purple and blue delight.

My heart sings in this season of new love
A chance to dream and bright hopes for tomorrow
A chance to try new things
Meet new people, do nice things

Holidays by the sea
With seagulls' wings
Their cry as they glide so high
In the new spring sky

Adults and children bobbing in the sea
Sandcastles built, an angel delight
Ice cream vans, willingly selling
Cones, choc-ice, lollies so tempting

Thank you Lord for a season so bright
And a world filled with your Heavenly delights
Mother and friends, flowers and birds
Are all gathered here for me
In your Heavenly world and spring!

Daniela Morbin

AWAKEN

Little brown seeds
Little brown brothers
Are you awake in the dark?
There you lie cosily
Close to each other
Waiting for the sound of the lark.

Waken the lark says
Waken and dress you
Put on your green coats so gay
Blue skies will welcome you
Sunshine will caress you
Waken 'tis morning 'tis May.

Alice Hemming

SNOWDROPS

Through frozen ground, laced with the white of frost,
Inhospitable, barren, dark and cold,
Green spears push up as if an elven host
Was marching from the depths to challenge winter's hold.
Pale spears of green, surely too frail to break
The stranglehold of dark and frozen earth,
Which, shroud-like, wrapped them, as through winter's wake
They waited for the day of their rebirth.
The slim pale buds first reach up to the light
Then hang their heads (each like a shivering bell)
Their first bold challenge melted into fright,
Their soundless overture to spring they tell.
And at the sight of such a fragile thing
We welcome winter's end and reach towards spring.

Eileen Burgess

HOMELESS

As summer wanes and nights begin
To chill, the nameless man now sleeps
On grill above a steady draught
Of warming air expelled from deep
Within a building housing large
Machine requiring constant flow
Of cooling breeze. At dawn he wakes
With stiffened joints and takes a swig
Of cider, chews a piece of bread
And shares his crusts with pigeons stood
Around in daily hope. But once
He ran a business in the north.
His wife was a lovely lass, his son
His pride and joy. Alas, they both
Were killed one dreadful day when car
Was hit by monster truck whose brakes
Had failed. From then his broken heart
Diverted mind from job in hand,
Until his bank foreclosed on loan.
So now he roughs it on his own
And views the world through different lens.
He needs the time to tame his grief
Before he's fit to work again.
So don't regard him with contempt,
For do you know how you would cope?
At least his pigeons show regard
As silent friends who don't condemn.
Perhaps they'll help restore belief
That life has purpose after all,
For now they help him face the day.

Henry Disney

MELODY OF SPRING

As dawn breaks on the horizon,
The blackbird greets the arrival of a new day,
I hear him warbling from the confines of our garden,
Beyond the floral curtains,
Hanging from the window of this sanctuary called home.

He calls to his mate, warbling,
With an extensive repertoire,
Awaiting her reply from some adjacent abode,
Interactive musical orchestrations of the maestro,
And his lady in her brown attire.

The songster trills his song so sweet,
Heralding the season spring in all its glory,
He rejoices in its arrival,
As skimming low across the garden,
His lyrical notes fill the air.

The tune that this our feathered friend chirps,
Spring is on the way,
And we pause 'midst our daily toil,
To reflect and delight in the blackbird on the bough,
And the melodic tunes that drift sweetly on our ear.

Alighting on the ground he seeks the unsuspecting worm,
Safe at present in its underground hideaway,
We witness the tilt of his head,
As his finely tuned hearing listens to vibrations,
Then with accuracy, the prey is located and retrieved.

The enchanting sounds of birdsong that fill the air,
Lyrical whistling on the breeze,
Remind us that once more we are witness to creation,
As we share the joy of reawakening,
Knowing that life and death has its season.

Ann G Wallace

SPRING WOOD

Spring Wood
even by name, not season
can be a new beginning;
it may not be a cure forever for stress
or the root treatment necessary for new birth
but just entering its enclosure
feeling its temporary peace descend
hearing the birds sing
noticing the distance between the drone of traffic
and the ever competitive encroaching world
brings God much nearer
re-inventing hope
a stepping stone.

Robert D Shooter

B-R-R-R-R-R!

B-r-r-r-r-r-r!
Walls creak as bitter cold
shrinks molecules.
Icy fingers trace crystalline
cryptograms on windowpanes
yet my blood runs warm.

B-r-r-r-r-r-r!
Wind digs wave-forms
in frozen snow
reminder of my frailty.
Showing tenacity of will
I push tired body against
bullying gales - a few freezing
steps at a time.
Toes & fingertips are numb.
Thoughts hang like icicles
from my mind.
I crawl mummified
yet my blood runs warm.

B-r-r-r-r-r-r!
Snow grows white walls.
I discern frost creeping like
divisional amoebas
on the rug. My toes curl
yet my blood runs warm.

So now you're here -
my *spring*. Smiling
you liquefy ice surrounding me
with a wave of your hand.
We move in Earth's rhythm
surrounded by the thaw.
Our blood runs hot!

Edward L Smith & Carmen M Pursifull

PERFECT START

It's getting warmer,
and I feel slightly better,
when it's brighter weather,
makes me feel quite cool,
it feels fresh,
the slight wind on my face,
it makes my heart race,
like you,

the frost has gone,
and now it's well on its way,
it'll fight another day,
not for a while,
you'll need sunglasses,
to put on that pretty nose,
don't forget those summer clothes,
they make me smile,

it gets lighter,
as the days get long,
feel good factor strong,
in my heart,
with you here,
and with the coming sun,
I feel my world is one,
the perfect start.

Chris Silvester

THE FIRST SNOWDROP

Kneeling in the coldness of dawn,
A hidden sister;
Concealed beneath her dark habit.
Head bent in prayer,
Her pious stance, though heartbreaking,
Holds promise of greatness
And eventual pride.
Pure white and somehow unformed,
This holy morning brings slow revelation -
Bleeds colour into her soul -
As she turns gently her face to the sun.

Suie Nettle

CHANGE

Life wavers through the tall grass and whistles through the air,
                                          between the rain
Buds are like emeralds on long spindly fingers.
The daffodils let their heads dip and sway in spring's warm breeze,
Like dancers with yellow streamers.

Summer brings a change, a vibrant array of colour,
Like the field now a golden ocean
Its tide ebbing back and forth
Not a single leaf flutters from its pedestal view
Of admiration for the flashes of colour, each one a shade varied.

Rust inhibits the trees of autumn, like an old nail left in
                                          dew-covered grass
Scarlet are the leaves, bloodstained as in battle.
The trees surrender, dropping their leaves in protest of the falling rain.

Winter turns them to skeleton shapes
Snow lays thick as though to bandage the once bloodied wounds
                                                  of each skeleton.
A change is needed, the wounds heal
As spring is inevitable.

B R Walker

SPRING SONG

From my window can be seen
Sunshine brightening up the scene
No swaying trees, nor waving grass
Too good this day, to let it pass
Too good to sit and wonder why
There are no clouds up in the sky
Why question, when the day looks fine
The air outside should be like wine
Don outdoor clothes and walking shoes
Now what direction shall I choose?
Perhaps I'll go and take a look
At the plants that grow beside the brook
Or skirting the fields to Blunden Hall
Past woodland glades where trees stand tall;
Or over the footbridge to Hawley woods
Where nature displays her changing moods
The woodpecker's tapping will always thrill
Like the sound of a small pneumatic drill
And then, the sweetest sound of all
That herald of spring, the cuckoo's call
A day, dull spirits to revive
And it is wonderful just to be alive!

Norrie Ferguson

COME SPRING

I think he sat:
He may have stood.
He chose the topmost place he could
And filled my ears with liquid sound.

The countryside was nearly white
Sun low, frost bright,
And he sang on as though he was
The one in the world with a message to tell.

He rang the air all up and down
The village street, without a care
For audience, response, or shift
Of wind that gently shook his perch.

A thrush; yes, almost certainly . . .
I thought of all the people getting up
Going to work, fighting the cold,
Hating Monday, feeling old.

And only a few would be surprised
By the joy from the throbbing
Body-filled torrent of feathered music
Out from the treetop falling, pouring.

John Brackenbury

THE RED LION, AVEBURY

I waited outside the pub
The spring sun shone brightly
But the wind was cold.
I thought of the Guinness and the stones,
Of the mystery surrounding me.
I tried not to look uncomfortable.

As I turned back to the door
My heart leapt as I saw a figure appear.
Unrecognised, you walked towards me.
I saw unimpeachable eyes and beautiful hair,
Dark skin
And a smile of unanswered questions.

I didn't need the confirmation
Of how I clearly felt.
I didn't need to be reminded
Of how beautiful you are.

Indy Clark

SPRING

Oh! Have you seen the cherry trees blossoming in the lane?
And have you smelt the primroses scenting the air again?
And have you seen the daffodils nodding their heads nearby,
Basking in the sunlight beneath a clear blue sky?
And does this mean that spring is here and winter's gone at last?
And shall we plant our seedlings and hope Jack Frost is past?
Or maybe we should wait awhile and not make too much haste,
In case the weather changes and all will go to waste.
Perhaps we'll settle for cutting the grass and wait a little longer
Until the clocks go forward and the sun's a little stronger.
For after all, it's only March and there's plenty of time, it's true.
So I'll just make the most of today by sharing it with you.

Jacqueline Hartnett

THERE'S A GLORY IN THE SPRINGTIME

There's a glory in the springtime
One cannot quite define;
Times of refreshing, sending now
Those shivers up one's spine!

One hears, one sees, one feels new life,
Reaching upward, spreading wide -
Fresh energy keeps pulsing through
Incoming like the tide!

Let's not miss out, let's celebrate,
Let's open wide the door
And so receive awareness new
Of gifts for us in store!

Anticipation is the key
And gratitude the crown
That bring an added lustre to
The glories we are shown.

Peter Spurgin

SO GREAT TO BEHOLD

We woke early this morning. It wasn't too cold.
The beginnings of springtime were great to behold.
We heard the birds singing, we saw the dawn break,
The blackbirds were waiting, the bread for to take.
Blue tits and coal tits enjoying the seed
When down flew the starlings with their usual greed.
The air smelt so good, we were glad to be there,
To give ourselves time to just stand and stare.

We've been gardening today. It wasn't too cold.
The beginnings of springtime were great to behold.
Clumps of white snowdrops; crocuses purple and gold.
Miniature Iris had begun to unfold.
Primulas, daffodils, the sweet tête-à-tête,
All helping, in their own small way, spring gardens to create.
Wonderful touches of colour, made bright by sun rays,
Bidding farewell to the winter greys.

We walked by the river. It wasn't too cold.
The beginnings of springtime were great to behold.
Coots and moorhens we saw on the way
And ducks all paired up, just waiting to lay.
The swans so noisy, in complete disarray,
They will lay their eggs from March to May.
The herons, so private, did not appear with the rest,
They will raise their chicks in last year's nest.
The beginnings of springtime, so great to behold,
This wonderful season will gradually unfold.

E Marcia Higgins

THE JOYS OF SPRING

Winter's still here – but not for long
Soon we'll hear the birds in song
Little shoots start peeping through
Snowdrops and crocuses - white and blue
Then we'll rise fresh as a breeze
No more shivering - no more freeze
What great joy spring does behold
Goodbye winter
Goodbye cold.

Theresa Griffiths

RIGHT ON TIME

Mother Nature . . . quite unique
Perfect timing from winter sleep
How do you know the time to grow
Tending each bud recovering from snow?

You changed the bleak bareness
You chose colours so right
How do you perfect this
Sometimes overnight?

Once barren and bare you breathed in the air
Giving bare twigs little buds galore
You give new shoots to soil and leaves to hedgerows
What else do you hold in store?

The birds are in chorus as they sing out at dawn
The grass starts to get longer and makes a fine lawn
Snowdrops get together, daffodils all line up and sway
A breeze makes rhythm for dancing, how clever to do it this way.

So thank you Mother Nature, but when your task is done
Could you paint the sky bright blue with lots of lovely sun?
Then when summer takes over you suddenly disappear
But we know we will see your work . . . each and every year.

Jo Hodson

LET NATURE SING

In the air the promise of new is near,
When in your eyes will be the joys of spring;
As those dark winter days now disappear
For the hungry cries of each newborn thing.
It is nigh for you springtime to give birth -
For the children of spring to grace the earth.

Olliver Charles

SPRING

After the bitter cold and lots of rain,
We feel so helpless which is such a shame,
So looking forward to the spring,
Always makes my heart sing.

Nowhere in the world I can say,
You can find climatic changes in one day
Because who knows when the sun will shine
In this beautiful England I call mine?

The birds and bees plus the squirrels and hedgehog
And our visitors include a cat and a dog.
Our garden is a paradise to behold
When the sun shines and the flowers bloom and glitter like gold.

To wake up to the dawn chorus in spring,
To a choir of musical chirps as the birds sing
Busily going on their way to the nest
Which they build for their family to feed and rest.

The buds bloom as they open and colour the garden and glow,
As they sway and produce a sweet aroma to show
That spring is here and hopes to stay
For as long as it takes to make it a lovely day.

So spring is the start of summertime,
When we enjoy a cold, long drink from oranges and lime,
Stepping stones to sunshine and happy days,
As love blossoms in spring in so many ways.

Beryl Sylvia Rusmanis

BLUEBELLS - THE HERALDS OF SPRING

Our town is noted for its beauty,
In 'Britain in Bloom' we rate good,
But to see nature in all her glory,
I suggest a walk thro' the wood.

What, climb Curly Hill! - I can hear it,
I couldn't do that, you declare,
So jump on a 'Hoppa' and just for a copper
He will take you safely there.

On the way you will see parts of our town,
Beyond where the river lies.
In a few minutes you're outside the woods
And oh, what a feast for the eyes!

You can turn to the right or the left,
Go uphill or down as you choose,
The ground is a carpet of flowers,
All shades of purples and blues.

See them once and they are never forgotten,
A sight that will stay in the mind
And God who cares for the sighted,
Also thinks of the blind.

As well as the beautiful colour,
The flowers are scented so sweet,
No perfume bought in Paris
This beautiful aroma can beat.

Just make the effort, do this trip once
And when in winter's gloom
You sit and picture the bluebells,
You'll smell their rich perfume.

Constance Vera Dewdney

EARLY MORNING MAGIC

The moon has been telling jokes all night.
In the morning we see
That the Earth has split her sides with laughing,
Stuffing leaks out,
Layers of wadding cover the fields,
Until seamstress sun extends her rays
And tucks it all back in.

A baby-eyed sky,
White muslin hangs across the sun,
Who is breathing through an open mouth,
Alternately sucking in then blowing out the veil.

The light is hazy, your eyes deceive.
Vision-edges blur like professional photos.
See through a magic lens, a fairy doorway,
A vertical halo of mystery.
Painting is pastel-smudged,
Paint only the scenes you love,
Smudge over the ugly.

Paula J Holt

WOODLAND IN WINTER

I leave behind mournful, bleak, open fields
Where fieldfares and redwings search for food,
Frozen hawthorn hedges visited by sparrows
Greedily feeding on dull red haws.
Amongst silent trees I enter the wood
Where dampness all around pervades the air
Whilst calls of birds are strangely amplified.
A grey squirrel runs along a bough
Watched by a robin, head cocked on one side.
On wet tree trunks are different colours
From the rich palette of moss and lichens
And red pustules of coral spot on fallen branches
Giving a whiff of slow decay
Reminding one of smells of mushroom sheds.
Beneath my feet the bulbs of bluebells sleep
Whilst acorns show the first signs of germination.
I pass the ground where in high summer I once made love
Today I have no appetite, squelching through twigs and leaves.
I break into the open, leaving behind the naked trees
And feel a warmth return to cold, damp bones
Fuelled by the distant lights of windows.

David A Garside

SPRING TO SUMMER

The trees stood stark, not in exotic places
But at the bottom of my garden.
The swallow song of winter is with us
Carving its message in snow!
Frost flakes fall down like muesli
Leaving a carpet of white in the snow!

The autumn is falling, like the dried up stream
In the clutch of frozen leaves.
The cornflaked ice is scattered on the
Hanging bank of low brushed trees.

The sobbing branches, weak as ice-drops
Dripping for the stream, skinny as small
As bird legs, its bark so ready to sneeze.

Winter is giving a strong message
For a smiling winter sun!
Freeze me not forever,
Let the spring to summer begin.

David Rosser

NATURE'S REVENGE

Slow, methodical, soaking drizzle,
nature's resolve for revenge on us.
The supposedly superior beings
Of this, our frequented planet.

With similar effect as life's problems
going unnoticed as in the background.
Yet always penetrating - eventually
often unavoidably almost as destined.

Comes feeling insignificant and hardly noticed,
yet seeps on through - to the skin.
Bringing our mood to down,
affecting every human emotion.

It's difficult to accept or believe
that something so slight,
so simple or unobtrusive,
could ever render such havoc.

Gary J Finlay

SEASONALLY AFFECTIVE DISORDER

The eye draws in the black
through ever growing tunnels
funnelling in the soot
of night, as hungry
pupils grow owl-wise
when grey grizzles around
the lining of the world.

On this side of the divide,
a hemisphere in darkness
mops up moonshine
gratefully and searches for the stars.

Creatures of the night
grope for the light in fires,
sparklers, whiz and bang,
anything to frighten off the things
that lurk in corners or in the shrouded
hedgerows endowed with
mystery, only because
crowded shadows, thickening
like cobbled scars in the gloom, drape
blackout blinds over the mind
in winter.

Diane Burrow

THE BELLS THAT TOLL ON A SUMMER'S DAY
(For Cathy 'Whene'r the sweet church bell peals over hill and dale, may Jesus Christ be praised.' Hymn by J H Clark, 1839-88)

The bells that toll
For You and me
We thank You, Lord
For joys so free
On a summer's day near Windsworth.
As boundless as the wind that blows
To bring their sound across the hill,
As once I heard a while since
Leaning on a gate to hear . . .
A bell that tolled from a hamlet church
Across the Devon pastures dear
At eventide,
A call to prayer.
My heart uplifts and swells
As I gaze on sparkling sea
And sun-drenched hills and dells
I feel the sense of peacefulness
From the music pealed by bells.

Anne Veronica Tisley

THE GOLDEN ORB

Up in the sky
The sun ablaze
Awakens slothful souls:
Through winter's gloom
And drear, damp days,
Lethargic they have been.

Now they attack the dust and dirt,
The cobwebs in the corners,
The carpets cleaned,
The curtains washed,
The vacuum cleaner buzzes:
For sunbeams mercilessly show
That dust lies all too thickly,
It's time to clean, to wash and shine,
It's what they call 'spring cleaning'.

The sound of mowers cutting grass,
Of clippers trimming hedges,
Metallic clang of tools
Long lying unattended.
For fresh green shoots
And growing plants
Are wakened by the sun,
So gardens, too,
Need tidying up
In readiness for summer.

All this commotion,
Rushing round,
Is caused by just one thing -
That bright gold orb up in the sky
That shows up imperfections!

Roma Davis

AN ANCIENT CHURCHYARD IN SPRING (CAVERSWALL)

Mid spring, in an ancient, rural churchyard
As the sun breaks through the dawn mist,
A scene as picturesque as an old postcard,
A place of quite contemplation and solitude
Bathed now in the morning sunshine.
The weathered tombstones lie askew,
Lichen and moss coated, worn inscriptions time obscured,
Surround by tussocks of uncut, strawy grass
Over untended, long forgotten graves.
The occupants into eternal sleep long passed,
But on these burial places long ago,
Relatives had come by in some long gone autumn,
To plant bulbs before the onset of the first snow.
Thereafter, in each consecutive spring
A golden, sun-stolen blessing they bring,
For daffodils spring forth; an Easter resurrection,
Their sunshine heads aglow, in zephyr winds' blow.
Simple kinds; the flowers small and unrefined
Country cousins, humble peasants wedded to the soil,
Vigorous and natural; a stronghold established without toil.
Brave and bold; thrust through the cold turf each spring,
Irrespective of what adversities the vernal season brings.
There they are, taking centre stage, the spring's superstars.
Like a dress rehearsal for Resurrection Day.
Long my these venerable varieties stay,
For each year they rise from their winter sleep
And on some April morn once more greet
The sleeping denizens of this sacred place,
These drifts of golden daffodils, bringing bliss,
Each with its radiant, ruff-surrounded face.

John Pegg

SPRING LAMBS

Spring lambs – such joy!
It isn't spring yet, and
My heart is full . . .
Two years ago . . .
Never can we forget
The pain still there,
The empty fields . . .
Empty no more
Life overwhelms us all,
My arms are full
Of trembling warmth
And trusting eyes
A watchful ewe moves closer -
She braved the cold
To bear her children:
So proud – my lambs!

My heart is full . . .

Carolyn Smith

RAINFALL

An assault of hyphens
Dart southerly leading
To more;
A huge exclamation
Marks the
Expected surprise,
The world crouches
In parentheses
Hopping between continuation
Dots from decay
To the fresh spelling out
Of new sentences,
Shifting emphases,
Leaping between paragraphs,
The emptiness is full
Of joyful simile:
Yellow fluffiness inhaled
And then standing, breathing,
Feeling that it's you
Willing it all,
The transition
Provides escape
But before one can draw
New breath,
A full stop.

Emily McLeod

SPRING PROMISE

Spring, did ever such a little word conjure up such a large picture
Of promises yet to come, of an end to the long, dreary winter
The yellow primroses along the hedgerows
The sea of bluebells in the wood
The buds on the trees bursting open
The sunshine being let into our lives again
And the feeling of regeneration
That comes with the new season

Spring is like no other season
Other seasons only mark the middle
Or end of nature's cycle
Only spring locks the door on our past troubles
And lets into our world the brightness and
Promise for a future free from the darkness and gloom of winter.

Phillipa Grundy

THE BREATH OF SPRING

The lake glistens
Under a luminous sky.
The robin sings the last
Of his winter's song.
Hedgerows give birth
To pink campion
And the shy primrose,
Their dark eyes
Weeping in the sun.

The child in me stirs
And shifts the weight
Of years, to allow
The breath of spring
To draw aside the veil
And allow my eyes
To see again.

Josephine Thomas

THE WALK

After my long sleep I wake refreshed
And nod to the sun.
The daffodils regally bow their heads
And whisper a quiet hello.

Crocuses of diverse hues
Welcome me as I pass
And greet me with an upright stance.
Reaching to touch the sky.

Delicate bells of snowdrops white
Tinkle and giggle with glee.
A magical, mystical wonderland
The earth finally free.

And the footmark of winter's boot
No longer suffocates the earth
Spring has released the captives
And there is joy in my heart.

Sabina Kelly

THE SERMON OF SPRING

In all hearts sung a sermon
A song for the birth of spring
And the voice thus sung of beauty
As the echo of winter fades
And thus came the seasonal messiah
Emanating from the soul of March
With the company of love and serenity
Amalgamating into a precious rapport

Flowers rise in a spiritual awakening
Pollinating the air with their love
Melting into the eye of the beholder
A liaison that very moment does praise
Birds migrated from the cage of winter
Navigating into the arms of a warmth
Flocks flew into a bosom of colour
That carpets the land with a dream

Thus a picture is painted of Heaven
Of a fairy tale that Mother Nature evokes
Spring saturated the heart with a freedom
Summoning grandeur to every dawn of its life
The year had brought spring to an audience
'Neath the splendour of an amorous sky
Spring whispered its sabbatical sermon
Into the heart of every eminent soul.

David Bridgewater

WINTER'S SLEEP

A stray chink of light
disturbs her sleep.
A promise of warmth,
bright spring days to come.
She snuggles deeper
into her duvet of white.
A late frost,
five minutes grace.
Nature's clock ticks,
surely soon she must awake.

Jefferson Hammond

OVERHEAD BUZZING CABLES

Weeping willows wept against
Degenerated barbed-wire fences.
Dandelion seeds ascended underneath
White, furry umbrellas in a hot
Afternoon sun, the same sun that
Was baking the diesel oil deep
Into the ageing sleepers.

Dereliction impressed itself on the
Landscape of the shunting yard.
Overgrown nettles irritated my
Bare ankles, whilst my sandals
Absorbed the heat from the uneven
Tarmac of the deserted path that
Runs adjacent to the railway sidings.

I wandered into the long grass, passing
A pair of defunct corduroy trousers and
An abstract-shaped piece of discarded
Linoleum. I lay down to the haunting
Sound of the overhead buzzing cables
And the distant clatter of the fifteen-twenty-three
Heading towards the outer suburbs.

Neville Anthony

APRIL IS THE CRUELLEST MONTH

A raindrop in suspense
balances its separation
from a leaf drops.

The leaf refreshed
leaps released

the raindrop
begins its descent
to the sea.

Leaf's ambition
and rain's energy
are innocent of envy
in the enigma
of being.

The wind pitilessly
severs the leaf
from its stem

the raindrop falls
by tree bark absorbed.

Each destiny foiled
by the enigma of definition
remaining undecyphered:

the cypher lies
by purity entombed.

Michael A Fenton

OLD WINTER'S DEATH!

Fields of sweet flowers
Will finally free
The wounded, paralysed soul!
Green spring life
Writing rhyming poetry
On grass for summer!
Old winter's death
Leaves a smile.
Walking in the sun;
It can soothe my worrying.
My nightmares are gone.
The sun is trying
To come out of the sadness
Caused by the black cloud;
The black cloud of winter.
The snow is melting
Off the tops of big tree logs!
Has springtime arrived?

Laraine Smith

GARDENER'S JOY

Snowdrops appear on white frosted lawns,
Soon daffodils will awake in golden glory born,
Crocus, hyacinths and tulips gay,
All appear soon after the first spring day.
Thrushes and blackbirds build their nest
They sit on eggs to hatch beneath their breast.
People are out preparing the ground
Digging and hoeing, everything must be sound.
They clean out the greenhouse and set their seeds,
Tend them with care, then pick out the weeds.
Summer has come, the garden's in its full beauty,
All thanks to the gardener doing one's duty.
I now sit out on a summer day,
The thrushes and blackbirds have hatched and are now out to play,
Watched by one crafty black cat,
I shooed him away, shouting to go catch a rat.
All my thanks to the seeds, my thanks to the flowers,
I can now sit in my garden and enjoy it for hours and hours.

Kathleen Gilboy

SPRING... A NEW BEGINNING

Silver dart pierces nature's canvas
Life springs forth with added zest
As new beginnings bring hope and joy
To a beleaguered world.
Fresh water - silver content,
Splashes across hungry stones:
Animals emerge from winter sleep
With deftly assured survival,
Thus the cycle continues
With early green and yellow
(Most virgin of colours)
Dominant once more . . .
It is a time of excitement
For this most passive of foes.

Arthur Pickles

SPRING IS IN THE AIR

Whether the sun is shining or the rain is pouring
Spring is in the air
And animals come out of hibernation
Including the bear.

Spring is in the air
And most of the animals start breeding.
Now the new lambs are feeding
Because of the four-leaf clover.

Spring is in the air
And shrubs and flowers come to life
And the March hares are looking for husbands or wives.
The days start getting longer
And the cold gets stronger.

Spring is in the air
And the mornings are brighter.
The evenings have become lighter
And plants have started to grow.
Now there are no more coverings of snow.

Coleen Bradshaw

SPRING

The spring is here,
There's green on the trees,
Buds ready to burst
In the warm spring breeze.

There's spring in the air
New life on its way,
Little innocent lambs
Spend their days in play.

With spring in full bloom
All those so early flowers
Remind us our gardens
Will need working on for hours!

Rowena Haley

STONY PATH

Walking on the stony path,
light shines from a cloudless sky
where coloured shards
from broken glass crushed
between stones - dazzle my eyes
in the shimmering sun.

Moving towards the big house
windowless and empty -
I trample on memories - where
once wine flowed into glasses,
arranged on long tables, after
men returned laden down with
wildlife from forest shoots.

Strips of light bursts out
of green flounces shaking and
dancing above my throbbing head
while perfumed clean air gives
back energy to my tired feet
as I plod along the stony path.

Mary Guckian

APRIL

Soft rain trickling down a pane
Of glass in quick-silver rivulets
Chasing each other, merging and diverging
In a serpentine dance.
Fickle April, as mischievous as ever
Shifts with sudden whim from sad
To glad mood,
And bleary sunshine blinks through
To mop up the tears,
So that all the burgeoning leafage stands out
Wet sparkling in bright spring colours
Like millions of fairy lights winking in the sun.

But not long before April veers again,
Darkening the fragile sky
To bruised and menacing indigo
And abrupt spears of steely rain
Attack the gentle earth with Wagnerian fury -
Until with yet another fancy
April's ill-humour changes
And the tentative emerging sun
Coaxes veils of vapour from the soaking grass
Suffusing all the edges
Like a watercolour painting.

Jean Atkinson

SPRING 1940

Cows, udder-deep in buttercup mud
Hooves and hocks suck, a squelching wail
Of sirens signalling bomb craters.
Butter-churning stomachs lurching.
Shrapnel condimented hay.
Autumn and not yet May.

Careless calves suck
Muck-spattered udders.
April showers of
Deadly incandescent flowers,
Children pick butterfly bombs
In the dawn of, whose finest hour?

How much mud and how much blood?
When churned and spread on, how many dead
Is enough?

I can still see those long-dead cows
And rows of crosses without end

Jack Major

THE BREATH OF SPRING

The hills above, still white with snow,
Stand silent and serene.
While in the valley far below,
The earth is fresh and green.
For spring had breathed upon the land,
Where snow had lain so deep.
And gently with a soft, warm hand,
Woke all from winter's sleep.

Tiny leaves of palest green
On every twig and bough,
Shoots of corn can now be seen
In dark brown fields of plough.
Soon clouds of golden daffodil
Will nod in warm spring breeze.
Until then the snowdrops will
Drift white amongst the trees.

From hibernation, cold and dark
Creatures will stir and yawn.
Sap will rise in dormant bark
As trees once more are born.
I felt the breath of spring today
Instead of winter chills.
Soon tiny lambs will frisk and play
On those green and sunny hills.

Marisa Greenaway

STOVER NATURE PARK

Wild tussocks intermingled with violets blue,
Stood at the base of the pine tree straight and true
And bursting buds on the willow tree
Stretched as far as the eye could see.
Mallard ducks swimming on the lake
Midst rushes tall, their food did take.
The sunny hours tempted us to stay
As spring was regaled in a new day.
Pussy willows turning green
Silver lined could still be seen.
Spring's rebirth hurried on its way
And gave to us a brand new day.
As all of nature's beauty stark
Was displayed for each in Stover Park.

Margaret Gurney

MUD

Trundling along the country roads
on a February day,
watching raindrops falling
not feeling very gay.
A field of pig loos caught my eye,
great sows rolling in the mud
and piglets gambolling and playing
oh so free!
I had to smile, it made my day
spring was in the air.
I bought a bird box
put it up - ten minutes later
our new tenants looked it over
'Des res' in the tree.
The two goldfinches and a long-tailed tit
came to feed.
The squirrel beat the washing line
assault course, to get his prize of nuts!
So much to look forward to once more
I just wish the world wasn't at war . . .

Liz Osmond

THE ROBIN

I paused to hear a robin sing
As I wandered down the lane.
Was he telling me spring had come
And that winter was on the wane?

I lingered awhile to hear the notes,
Trembling on the sunny air.
Smiling, just to hear his joy,
Perched on a branch, greenly fair.

He stared at me with sparkling eyes,
'Admire my song,' he seemed to say,
As I stood there, hearing his tune.
Then with a nod, he flew away.

Rose-Marie Bonnevier

SPRING IS IN THE AIR

The rich black soil is free from frost
Gurgling ditches freely flow
Now winter's icy tentacles
Have been released by sunshine's glow.

Our garden slowly wakes from sleep.
Snowdrops, then the daffodils
Lift up our hearts with sheer delight
Sun's warmth will banish winter chills.

The colourful cock pheasant struts
Advertising for a mate.
He calls in his imperious way
Inviting them to procreate.

The blue tits build their fluff-lined nests
Blackbirds and the cooing dove
With trilling chaffinch gladly join
The dawn chorus in songs of love.

Muriel Berry

SPRING SYMPHONY

Sunlight dancing on rain-kissed leaves
Lights a chandelier in nature's ballroom
On a carpet of velvet green
Golden trumpets herald the awakening season
Of rebirth.

Snow flowers cloaked in a mantle
Of frosted silk
Glisten as pearls in the morning sun
Trees wearing gowns of pink satin
Whisper softly as they feel nature's music
Breathe life into their soul.

A chorus of feathered voices
Bring harmony and joy with songs
That flow with the rhythm of the trees
Cascading waters refresh the spirit
As the air is filled with
Spring's orchestral magic.

Carole Harradence

THE STIRRING OF SPRING

When winter sometimes seems so long
When nights are darker and days so short
We miss the sun, the brightness of the day
When it seems there is only rain

We see our trees so bare after cold winds have stripped them
We are unable to go out and about
For one reason or another
When the feeling of loneliness steals in

Wondering if the winter will ever end
The longing to feel the warmth of the sun
But let us take a closer look to see
The stirring of the spring

As the earth warms up
Tiny bulbs bursting forth into view
The crocuses so small but beautiful to behold
Pushing their way from the cold earth
To the warmth above

We see a host of golden daffodils
Bright sky blue flowers
Deep pink and vibrant red
They brighten the cloudiest day
And the fragrance making this world
A sweeter smelling place

It reminds me of God's love
How he turns a cold heart to the warmth of his love
The beauty of his love reminds me of a flower
As the buds unfold revealing the beauty
The beauty of the colour within

The deep, deep beauty that resembles God's love
When it blooms in our hearts
We can't see his love but then God touches our heart
It will burst forth filling all the joys within

Then we see the beauty of his love
Like an everlasting flower in full bloom.

Eira Chapman

MARCH WINDS

Invisible menace,
Born of the air,
You snatch my clothes,
And mess my hair!

'It's my job!'
You said and grinned,
Such a spiteful pest,
That keen March wind!

Kerri Fordham

AUTUMN FEVER

Subtlety and vibrancy in presentation,
an integration of different colours
or solemnity of bare branches
stripped of their majestic title,
the essence of character, a true self.
The breakaway of enlightening leaves
the silence of bereft flowers
the sorrow of stubborn dusk
and a half-closed deceived eye.
The chirping birds and morning sky
It is no more, it is no more.

Samina Amjad

GREEN-LACED OASIS

Spring, the green-laced oasis.
The song from nature
which buds within the bush.
A rushing stream,
pregnant with life
that thunders around us
in its high-pitched song.
From frog of riverbank
to singing bird.
The tensions of life released
among the glittered jewels
of understanding.
The captured scene of future joys
that stay at our side
in this summer of contentment.
The marriage with the ring,
all moments looked upon
from nature's sprung tree
which drifts away to new horizons
on the shaped branch of prosperity.

Roger Thornton

SUNFLOWER

A field of yellow flowers beckon
each yellow peach petal, each in sharp profusion
'gainst a halcyon sky of blue
igniting the sultry August air
radiant rays pierce
the pinnacles of Heaven
like an army of soldiers
with warm round brown faded faces
standing still like silent golden giants
elongated to touch the summer sun
row upon row they sprung and hung suspended
ever upwards pointing, piercing
bright spikes of burnished gold and brown . . .

But flowers do bloom in Baldock
Fields of gold forever
In memories, mists of time ticking
I will remember
sunbursts and a cloudburst of colour.

Ruby Debnam

HILLS

Far away, the hills rise
Places of mystery and enchantments
Prehistoric burial chambers
Copses, grain fields, spinneys
Deer browse in the warm sun
Kites wheel, rabbits run in fields
Red poppies spring up in cornfields
White woodruff in orchards,
Mauve thistles 'neath English oaks
Saxon churches, thatched cottages
Imaginations set free, dreams of escape
Peace and tranquillity, solitude and song
Winding country lanes, cow parsley,
Canopies of rich beech leaves,
Blue skies washed by spring rains
Summer stands at the gateway.

Janet Eirwen Smith

WONDERS OF THE DEEP

Deep down beneath the sea
There're many wonders to behold.
Fish of many shapes and sizes
Colours of the rainbow
Are a delight to see
Glowing in the coral.
Multi plants do grow
While small creatures, weave to and fro
The divers are amazed
To see the sunken galleon
Coated with barnacles and seaweed
A home for many fish
And in the sand, a sea chest
A treasure trove of golden coins
From days gone by
Wealth beyond their wildest dreams.

A Higham

PAINTINGS IN THE CLOUDS

Looking out of my window,
Staring into space,
Watching the clouds
Drift along,
Forming different shapes.
I see men, women and children
With a happy smiling face.
There are mountains, trees
And pale blue lakes.
A walrus, seals, even an
Elephant shape.
Oh now I see a Cavalier,
White shirt with frills of lace.
An old Victorian gentleman,
A stern look upon his face.
It makes me deeply wonder
Are all these images in space
Or is it my imagination.
For I'd dearly love to paint
And if I were an artist
Out of the clouds I'd paint.
My paintings would be more beautiful
Than anyone could ever paint.

Doreen Petherick Cox

SUMMER STORM

Quiet stillness wraps around weary body, fresh breeze sneaks through open window. Evening perfume floats effortlessly from twilight garden, leaves rustle gently, teasing flying insects. Windy whispers sway curtain, strange scratchy noises interrupt dozy dream, wings flutter, bouncing feathery echoes, toward sleepy ears. Soft balmy breeze wafts ghostly illusion.
Stretching full length, tuck hands under cosy pillow. Delight summer evening brings.
Squabbling tom cats, hiss angry remark, buzzing creatures, splatter windowpane, tiny wings cling onto ivy branches, daintily casting phantom shadow. Moonlight silhouettes mirrored image dancing from wall to wall.
Storm clouds gather, clear night sky cools. Strong wind rattles open window, curtains zigzag. Raindrops pitter-patter oozing summer grassy smells, chilly draft bathes sleepy face, sudden freshness fills stuffy room. Every human sense drinks passionately, nature's pleasure. Lashing rain pounds swooping downward, splashing patio stone, thunder rumbles, lightning strikes earthward bomb. Raging wrath nature surge, how profound, how awesome. Blind fury. Angels singing, God clanging cymbals.
I slept with Mother Nature tonight.

Ann Hathaway

INTEGRITY

Honest twist of swollen rivers true in
currents swayed by the brush of a broom
swept away.
Lifelong soul arranges poverty for
knowing truth unsold in the bare marketplace
bestrewn by cabbage leaves yellow;
green veins pass spirit on level dunes sandy
in the lone of free waves which bounce echo
of white horses intense of feelings twisted
like spring toil of labour hard foraged
from sensual eruption of flowing grace.
Emotional tendency condemned on trial of
twelve gongs sounding out the Town Crier
shouting hollow nerve discerned.
Basic tears wept in wild profusion call
symphonic hope aware of nearness sown in
harvest of golden bloodstream, drowned by
lies told for corn flashed on fields
ingrained by the capillaries of a perfect
protection of armour shining in moonbeams
aglow with moths abuzz.
The dream of niceness in treacle grease
dispels the idea of contract tort bespoken
in oral tribute which adventure dashes
forward in purple haze, crested on silver
horizons blessed.
By forethought known by psychic belief
seeking intense knowledge of outer space
the planet of sincerity turns sharp retort
of plain speaking choral in voice though
tormented by choice of fibbers called to

the bar of ales, gleeful in vacuum spirit
empty of glasses full with truthful voice
while sponges suck toffee on the palate of tongues
screaming for love.

Doug Ramsay

SPECTRES VAPID

On a breezy afternoon - falls red, brown, yellow leaves
From dying decaying dark barked branches of overcrowded trees
Into leafy mulch careless feet fling up - soon to be washed away -
The smallest scrap.
If in rain falling from grey sky cloudy memory comes
If rain stays - like the vapours of ghosts - not ready to
Leave Earth - for contend I not thee thy presence.
Stay then these shades a while - in death of the passing year
If spectres vapid - some purpose mark thee
Of death's pallor found; or death's mask wear; or death's shroud fitted
To be one with death yet still be living.

C J Bayless

LISTEN AND LOOK!

The poet sees as the artist sees
Earth's beauty all around.
Earth's beauty, it comes alive
In shadow, light and sound.
And we all see as time goes by
A very different view
Too each there will be
Something new to see
Special for me and you.

Life is our own picture book
And so with each new day
The artist will guide us along
And the poet will write
In verse and song,
So, listen and look
Enjoy each new day,
Praying that terror and war
Will never take this away.

Dorothy J White

FOR EYES THAT DON'T SEE

For the eyes that see only night
Senses you know please share my sight
Come journey with me through leafy lanes
Where sunbeams form golden chains
Past tiny cottages draped in autumn's shades
Now bright summer flowers pale and fade

Over mountains majestic in size and wonder
Where clouds turn black holding fists of thunder
Follow sparkling rivers to valley floors
Then onto the expanse of patchwork moors
Forests of paintbox pines reach to the sky
Broad leaf trees turning to colours of fire

Meandering roadways form a glittering hue
As sunbeams dance on morning dew
Arching rainbows from the rains of September
Cobwebs glistening, ruby berries to remember

Warm breezes now blow with autumn's warning
Soon leaves will dance to winter's squalling
Granite-grey walls of castle and tower
Churches of old where the clock strikes each hour

So do please come with me
Share my sight
For I hold dear all these memories
As I close my eyes to the night.

Susan E Roffey

BESIDE THE SHORE

I sat beside the sea today
    And watched its sombre hue,
Above the windswept, autumn sky
    A delicate tint of blue.
Unkempt the grass of sand dunes
    Lurched in drunken gait
While lace, in ribbons, edged the sea
    In wild and careless state.
Sand in golden billows
    Rushed reckless o'er the shore,
Pursued by gusts of feckless wind
    Which also seemed to draw
Puffs of cloud across the sky
    At swiftly moving pace
To toss them, then, with carelessness
    T'wards any vacant space.
The sun, with chilly brilliance,
    Gazed upon the scene
Creating depth and beauty,
    And shadows for my dreams.
A seagull, preening daintily
    Where damp sand met the sea,
Favoured me a little while
    With his company.
I mused until the scudding clouds
    With peach began to glow
Then, turning saw the setting sun
    Was sinking very low.
Dying now, the autumn day
    Was slowly stripped of light,
As, to the last aloof and chill,
    The sun slipped out of sight.

Valerie L Warsop

Morning Glory

The glory of it.
Its supreme eminence
as it sweeps across in front of you.
Its blue beauty basks you in its glory.
The fireball's fingers lick
over the tops of trees
and meet the brilliant blue, embracing it,
smothering it with its ferocious heat.
Warming the hearts of the onlookers
as they stand and gaze at its beauty, drawn
to this wonder of nature.
A phenomenon of time
that comes upon us every day, without fail.
Enchanting.
Majestic.
Beautiful.

Nicky Ridsdale

COUNTRY WALKS

It gives me a thrill with the scent from the trees
and is just like a medicine which puts one at ease.
To walk through the woods by a well-worn track
then stop for a coffee from the pack on your back.

I love here the solitude so calm and serene
with no noise of traffic to alter the scene.
The birds chirping gaily from high in the pines
the wild flowers all blooming their colours divine.

The rabbits are nibbling at tender green shoots
but are off like a shot at the sound of a foot.
Squirrels are leaping about in the branches
with skilled acrobatics or something that's fancy.

I get joy from the freedom you find in the wood
as it gives me much pleasure which can only be good.
I love the fresh air which is free of pollution
and for any weak chests this can be the solution.

I take a note book or pad on all of my treks
and write of my adventure with this as a check.
This keeps in remembrance of the days I have spent
trekking the woods which to me is Heaven sent.

Lachlan Taylor

TULIPOMANIA

Flower of the east
speculative hysteria
Dutch seventeenth century
Tulipomania

Twenty-first century
fantasising gardener
mad about tulips
is Tulipomaniac?

fleshy brown bulb
tight tunic sheath
palmed into
winter's womb slumber

May green emerging
stem snakes erect
sharp leaves enfold
viperish bud swells

fluted flower bells
but no bud bursts
nor calix collars
tulip's smooth stalk

petal folds flush
green goblet fills
pumping pink pigment
to pert petal tips

red satin petals
pout to reveal
black silk stamens
pulchritudinous pistil

Seventeenth century
Tulipomaniac
traded all worldly goods
for one tulip bulb.

Twenty-first century
fantasising gardener
goes catalogue crazy
has Tulipomania?

Val Plant

THE EDEN PROJECT

The clay was quarried from the pit for over a century,
At the end of its useful life it became part of the scenery,
In this massive steep-sided unstable clay pit.
With the power of man and nature, came the Eden Project.
After excavating and planning, Eden is now a unique global garden.
An oasis, where man and nature has created a project of distinction.
Winding paths lead down from the Visitor Centre
Into a maze of gardens and flowers, colourful and spectacular
Landscaped gardens of herbs, plants, shrubs and trees,
And plants of every variety in biomes from far away countries.
In a massive biome, tropical plants and flowers grow in
									humid conditions.
With exotic birds, a waterfall crashing down from top to bottom.
Paths wind up through the biomes to platform levels
Where people can look down, the view is unforgettable.
At the pit base, seats face an open air theatre,
A beautiful setting for Cornish choirs and concerts.
People stroll the winding paths, see statues of Adam and Eve,
Visit gift shops and restaurants, have a pasty, a cup of tea.
Thousands of people from around the world.
Visit the Eden Project in wild and beautiful Cornwall.
Looking down from the Visitor Centre the view is incredible.
Sparkling biomes, moving train, colourful flags, gardens and people.
Within the soil and granite walls of a Cornish clay pit
Emerges another wonder of the world, 'The Eden Project'.

Lorna June Burdon

TREES

Dynamic and tall in their splendour they stand
The sycamore, oak and the ash
Silver birch wave tiny leaves in the breeze
Gentle winds rustle invading their dreams
The onset of spring with warm sunshine
And people relax to escape
The winter that's taken its toll now I fear
As now we must listen and wait
Beautiful and proud they reach for the sky
In splendour and elegant grace
And leaves that dripped with tears of joy
The spring buds burst into place
Ready for the summer to give shelter to the birds
Selecting a nest for their brood
Protecting the nestlings from changes unseen
As each season changes the mood
Butterflies taking their first maiden flight
The creatures in woodland and field unite
Then over the ponds dragonflies hover
With wings iridescent and blue
Welcoming skies that can change any time
To make colours of a different hue
Such beauty is all around us
If we only take time to look
For some day I feel all this will be gone
With concrete instead of the trees
Then the beauty of God's creations
Will be yours and mine no more
As shattered dreams and tear-filled eyes
I love and will try to protect
My beloved countryside.

Irene Siviour

Natural Break
(However much we encroach upon the world of nature - with our experiments and emissions - it still retains the power to heal itself, to maintain an equilibrium. It was here before us and, despite what we do, it will outlast us.)

The reeds bend in frozen attitudes of prayer,
    clasped in a moment of faithful inattention
        across this silent meadow,
    held fast by the cruel north wind,
dark crows circling in raucous vigil
    on its gusting ice streams high above the congregation,
    caught in suspended animation
        thin fish hang across the river stones
            below an arched roof of ice,
    seeking anything to prolong life
        in the cold echoes of their shadow-world,
    in this cathedral of expectancy,
thin fossil shapes over exposed by a blinding silver sun -
a shoal of starved penitents gaping noiselessly,
    waiting . . . waiting . . . for communion.

The tracks in the snow thread a pepper-dot course
    across a hillside of ancient gorse . . .
Eyes wide and alert, the fox and the doe stiffen,
    upset by premonition.
In a flurry of ice and dusty snow a short eared owl
    flaps into the clouds with an undignified howl,
        as a line of light sears the under sky,
    hunted by an ear-splitting cry
        two fighter jets streak across the valley floor,
filling its walls with their demonic roar . . .

A shapeless horror seizing the countryside,
   shakes the dignity from its antlered hide
      and in the slow moments of aftershock
     a shell case screams to earth with the heat of molten rock,
targets the river in the frozen meadow,
   smashes its ice,
   scorches its depths,
      pinions a fine old carp
      to the weed-bearded bed . . .
sending a column of water high into the frosty air
tearing the roots of riverside trees like a comb pulling hair

   The meadow shudders beneath this callous tyranny . . .
While, old as the hills, cold as the snow,
forces which lie at the heart of storms
   whose sleeping twitches cause mountains to fall
awake in the darkness of the earth below
      sending out fingers through the meadow's root and sinew,
   adjusting, balancing, building anew . . .
The hills absorb the echoes,
   muffle the indignant cackling of the crows
      and settle back into the winter slow;
   profaned yet splendid nonetheless,
the reeds bend in frozen attitudes of care . . .

James Thomson

NATURE'S VOICES

The roar of great Niagara,
And the falls of Iguazu,
Show us with strength and energy
What water power can do.
Their voices are so loud and strong
By night as well as day,
Their angry roaring can be heard
For many miles away.
Nature has many voices,
The sweet song of the lark
When in the morn ascending
And the owl's hoot after dark.
The vixen's night-time screaming,
The stock dove's gentle coo,
And the rooster's morning serenade
Of cock-a-doodle doo.
The wind sings in the woodland trees,
And chattering loud the brook,
Soft sighing is the gentle breeze,
Loud cawing of the rook.
All these are nature's voices,
We hear as seasons fly,
But the sweetest sound of human voice
Is a mother's lullaby.

Margaret B Baguley

CAVERN OF WEEDS . . . THE PIKE

The jaws hooked clamp and fangs,
Not to be changed at this date;
A life subdued to its instrument;
The gills kneading quietly, and the pectorals.

Three over two, we kept behind glass,
And four under two and a haft; fed fry to them . . .
Suddenly there was two across four, finally one.
Jungled in weeds; three inches, maybe four, within the pike.

With a sag belly and the grin it was born with.
And indeed they spare nobody.
Two, four, and six pounds each, over the willow-herb . . . the pike.
High and dry and dead, over two feet long plus.

One jammed past its gills down the other's gullet:
The outside eye stared: as a vice locks; cavern of weeds the pike
The same iron in this eye; catch me as you can,
Though its film shrank in death.

Pike, three inches long, perfect catch.
Pike in all parts, green tigering the gold.
Pike killers from the eggs; the malevolent aged grin.
They dance on the surface among the host of flies.

Or move, stunned by their own grandeur,
Over a bed of emerald, silhouette over the way of water.
Of submarine delicacy and horror, of many pikes there.
A hundred feet long in their world, but together.

In ponds, under the heat-struck lily pads . . . the pike.
Gloom of their stillness: *watching the hooks.*
Logged on last year's black leaves, watching upwards.
Or hung in an amber cavern of weeds . . . the pike.

Viv Lionel Borer

WHERE WILL IT END?

We see life passing,
Earth shifting
The sun getting hotter,
The ozone hole bigger.

Man does not know when to stop,
Polluting everything in his path,
Seas . . . rivers,
Trees dying.
Forests and animals,
Few and far between.

Man made fibres,
Chemicals producing nasties . . . seeping into the ground
Or being dumped.

When will it end, till life runs out,
Or Earth is gone.

Aline McInnes Ross

WORLD OF CONFLICT

The wind whistles through the screaming trees
Of a thousand politicians broken promises
Of sins not forgiven in Earth's hour of need
The children of perdition wail in anguish
At faded empire's hour of pity
At man's inhumanity to man
The warlords gather like buzzards
Circling greed in increasing deceit
The planet is polluted beyond redemption
Mankind has burned a hole
In the prospectors pan of gold
Only to sift hopelessly weeds of wrath
As the hangman of despair lurks fearfully
Towards death and destruction
As the chimes of freedom
Tingle disrespectfully the hope of the orphan child
Born out of a troubled world
And a blood tainted future.

Finnan Boyle

THE WORLD

The world is the most precious thing
Where little buttercups and roses grow
And where the animals frolic in the outside breeze
Where the human children play with nature
As it grows day by day
Nature is a very delicate thing
Of its special powers that it holds deep inside
The world might be polluted with pollutants
Or filled with robbers and stabbers
But the world, my little world
Is mine alone
Which I hold and treasure forever

Sheun Oshinbolu (10)

THE PRIDE AND THE PASSION

Rolling hills ablaze

Gold cups on a silver platter,
carried on wings of angels
that nations may toast
each other, safely come
to harbour

Rolling hills ablaze

Now glowing purple, now
flickering white, like the face
of a dreamer prospecting
for gold, fuelling native
tales of old

Rolling hills ablaze

Children of fire, anxious
to light world and word
with candles of peace;
California's pride, its
poppies

R N Taber

COASTLINE

Surf splashes quietly, foamy,
lapping gently across the beach.
Bubbly, transient, soothing.
Gushing frothily like excess lager,
oozing down the sides of a glass.

Molluscs glimmer, darting vibrantly,
secreted by sand and shale,
flashing cheekily against the sky.
Twinkling radiantly through solar rays,
basking in the smiling sunshine.

Tumble-down cafes litter the prom,
paint scaling from flaking woodwork.
Menu boards stand adrift, defiant,
fighting the fight forlornly.
Wilting to the rigours of time.

Oil rigs dominate the skyline.
Sombre, gothic, menacing,
stalked by a circling sea plane.
Seagulls squawk nervously, startled,
keeping time to the engine's drone.

A dog stares, eyeing quizzically,
stick embedded between its teeth.
Whistles pierce, slicing through the air.
Dutifully it trudges forward,
braving the shimmering heat haze.

Paul Kelly

Autumnal

Swans that fly across our skies
Talk as they go those graceful birds
Not one not two but a flock
A sight to see at autumn time

Autumnal is the word I seek
That time of year for warmer climates
Little birds that summer here
Must fly south for wintertime

I wish you safety, upon your flight
Strong wings, that will carry you home
Come back next year little birds
I'll wait till then, my little friends

Now is the time to see
Different swans upon our shores
They winter here in our land
So regal are these graceful birds

When seasons come and go
Lives are changed once again
Now we see our world
In shades of yellow, red and brown

I have the time to sit and stare
This perfect world so beautiful
With birds that fly across our skies
This pleasure given, insurmountable

I love this land in which we live.

Carole A Cleverdon

SEE OF ARRAY

Consoled as where ever, an oft distant shore,
The black clouds of morn, there contain,
Those sunbeams, come few,
To beginning, are through,
Who could ask? There but ever, for more,
A close knit assemble, the dewdrops in falling,
The rain seems as far from that cloud,
As it wanders its way,
To a gathered array,
Will the clasp be contained of its shroud,
Those skies of Heaven, they stretch to be far,
Across yonder blue there, the sun rays display,
Much further as such,
The space is supreme,
An eternal, begotten, portray,
Heavenly bodies in their race, o'er our time,
Would climb of their heights, way beyond,
The colour of darkness.
In the sea, there gone by,
Is past sense, oft glorious remind,
That life, can drift on, however its lie,
The dawn come back the dusk, there became,
As travel moreover,
A grasp of the day,
And its following task will imply,
Asteroids travel, you could pick them as one,
By lightning their footsteps along,
The gather's of rubble,
And spacely debris,
Or moon beams, of Heaven, belong.

Hugh Campbell

AESTHETIC SETTING

The east wind is rising above the hill, dividing us from town
We can hear the sound of the train in the coast tunnel
The view to Hatton's rocks is beautiful.
It's a different part of the Earth we live in
Far away from noise, pollution and problem
Out here there is peace
The wind is soothing
As it rushes through the trees -
Sycamore leaves rustling.
The hill is blue, the bog-brown, and the distant fields, a huey green.
Nature is colourful
The harvest is ripening
I am happy
At 15.

Noel Thaddeus Lawler

WHERE I LOVE TO BE

Here on the high cliffs
Is where I love to be,
Looking out to sea,
Where the wild wind blows free.

Watching the waves
Roll and crash,
As the froth bubbles
On the rocks crash and smash!

Rolling back
To surge again furiously,
The moon pulls the tides
And the sea pulls me.

I hear the seagulls calling,
See them dipping and diving,
With each new gust
My thrills are arriving.

With hair flying,
Fresh and bracing,
I'm standing strong,
The elements facing.

Here on the high cliffs
Is where I love to be,
Looking out to the sea,
Where the wild wind blows free.

Carol Ann Darling

FLOWERS IN THE SPRINGTIME

The park looks so beautiful today,
The blossoms all aglow,
Almond, currant, lilac and cherry,
Adorn the winding lane.

Daffodils - so warm and so golden,
Tulips as bright as the day,
The singing birds herald the break of day,
Grass twinkles with the dew of the morn.

The sun shines high in the noon day,
The trees burst out into leaf,
At eventide the sun sinks deep in the sky
To waken our loved ones 'neath another sky.

Nature is so wonderful
Wonderful to behold.

Janet Cavill

FEELING MY SENSES

I love the elements of nature
I've done it all my life
It makes me feel young again
Like snowflakes upon my face
Feeling like a child again
Playing my favourite game.

Feel the breeze blow gently
Upon your face
See a bird soaring through the air
Hear a bird sing its dawn chorus
To the brand new day

Taste the raindrops upon your tongue
Listen to the breaking of a brand new day
Touch the petals of a newly
Opened flower
Smell the fragrance of a flowering rose

And remember how it felt
When you smiled.

Christine Taylor

NATURE'S BOUNTY

The tinkle of the little stream,
Like a piano, melody plays,
The warmth of the beating sun,
A blanket, summer days.

Overhead, a chorus from,
Feathered friends in tree;
Paradise, enveloping,
All around me.

Fresh air smell, nectar,
Brings sweet caressing high,
From meadow flowers, blooming,
Reaching for the sky.

Beneath me, my cushion,
Of green, sweet smelling grass,
Untold joys to 'townies',
Nature's bounty on mass.

I don't want to go now,
Though my heart has had its fill;
But I am now addicted,
To this heavenly countryside pill.

There's no better place to be,
Away from traffic and fumes,
But sadly I must go now,
As night-time, it looms.

But I'll not be gone far,
Just to my caravan,
I'll return on the morrow,
On my holiday, while I can.

D Parry

FREEDOM

To feel as free as a bird in flight
With graceful movements of perfect flow,
And to gently glide with vision great,
A landing safely on earth below.

A lofty tree would then be my home
With delicate leaves of perfect shade,
A safe shelter from a rain-swept sky
Until angry clouds would seem to fade.

Then to view the earth from height so great
And scan the landscape of magnitude,
A feeling of interrupted space
Making descent in search of food.

Then the hasty lift-off from the ground
To my tree of sanctuary above,
There the hum-drum noise of traffic drowned
In my perfect haven that I love.

But then if my life there all alone
Seemed as lonely as a life could be,
I would hope, one day, another bird
Would find its home in my chosen tree.

If some day the friends that flew abroad
Could decide our home is their home too,
When they returned we would celebrate,
With lilting songs 'neath skies of blue.

At the break of dawn, in early morn
We'd welcome sweetly, one another,
Explaining how happy we would be
Sharing God's gifts, maybe forever.

Irene Grahame

THE RIDGEWAY

There is a favourite place where I escape sometimes.
This ancient green road runs towards the west
from Chilterns to Berkshire downs to Wiltshire green
(but never in the other direction!)
Here I can find peace and joy and beauty
in solitude and quiet, never loneliness,
and lift my spirit up to higher spheres.
All I can hear are breezes through the trees,
great clumps of beech that stand aloof and dark.
A sky-lark rises over cornfields, song aloft,
hovering above a nest so well concealed,
that I must tread more carefully than usual.
Here and there a glimpse of deer or hare
show perfect harmony of form and colour.
Only a distant fleeting train that snakes
through chequered fields below, returns one's mind
to reality of on-going living and the daily grind.
To the far west, the glorious comforting Cotswolds;
to north, blue misty views of Oxford's Shotover.
Sometimes I meet an earnest, back-packed man
with muddy, well-worn boots and sturdy stick.
Exchange of nods and cheery morning smiles
sufficient - humans are irrelevant up here!
The early drovers with their woolly flocks
were first to use this ancient English road,
now rutted, full of rain in winter, mud in spring,
and fringed with narrow strips of splashed, worn grass,
while further back, long copses where the pheasants hide,
and wild things undisturbed, get on with life.

J M Gardener

THE CROCUS

It's such a simple flower
Of no magnitude.
Its colours bright,
But magnified a thousandfold
By its wintry setting.
A small flower,
But tall against the sleeping grass.
It has no significance.
Except that of a stamp on a letter.
A little colour on a plain background.
But heralding good news,
News of a birth.
A rebirth of spring,
A whiff of summer
And a continuance
Of Earth's eternal cycling.

Harry Lyons

STARS

Billions of little diamond worlds
Dusting the darkness with light
The fusion of two complete opposites
Forming a picture so bright.

An historic statue each one forms
Moulded from struggle and strife
Splendidly showing the advantage
Of a totally unselfish life.

Removed from their past by force
They doggedly refuse to succumb
This display of their resilience
Is seldom equalled by none.

I Mackenzie

Autumn

The sunless rivers rest
They have earned their sleep
The waters run freely
As they begin to weep
No more flowers bloom
No more fields of corn
The earth rests for it needs it
Until another dawn.

The last nightingale sings
Its last sad song
The skies look pale
For now it will not be long
Grey clouds come
And so does the rain
No more rich, green grass.

Deep purple skies above
Leafless branches reach out like hands.
It's time when the earth
Rests its attractive lands.
Yet soon the skies will pale even more
And the air will get even colder
And the earth's cold corpse
Will curl up as it grows ever older.

Marc Shemmans

SOARING HIGH

Soaring high, swooping and swaying
Majestically through the air
Gliding effortlessly
Crying relentlessly
Hunger driven
Riding the air

Such beauty, such perfection
Such raw instinct
Watching and swooping on its prey
No guilt, no sorrow, no pain
The majestic eagle soars

Agnes Neeson

CLEMATIS

Exquisite petalled octet on a flower,
Each whorl purple-striped to centre,
It cascades over garden arch,
A tribute to Heaven's painter!

In winter each thin twig was bare,
No hint of ever growing,
Yet spring's healing warmth of sun
Sent myriad plump buds showing.

Then miracle of spring apparent,
Each bud unfurled so slowly,
Thrusting forth its pointed star,
Gems from the Gardener Holy!

Pat Heppel

THE WINDYLEHOO!

The wind is screaming in the west, swift as a shooting star - *warra, wharo, whoo, warrawaa*
Now button up your thickest coat - *lash down* your woolly hat, here on the slidy steepy slope, don't let your covers flap
The wind whistles at my back, I turn - it makes me slow - it shivers, my ears, flaps my hair - *wharroh,* watch it blow!
There's a light line in the heaving sky - whilst the moving clouds run black
The windy whirls run ringlets round, birds come propelled back - *Wheeawhoo,* the hurricane breath proclaims - o'er Wheddon Cross and Cutcombe the windywhoo it reigns -
The rooks they travel backwards, and fail to claim a tree - arrow fleet in down draft - hillside slippery -
Gliding down the slipstream - little bird let go - the whooshing world belongs to us, in it, we must flow -
Wharra wharra whoo - wharra-wharra-wharra - the wind is screaming in the west, howling near and far, heaving at both hedge and flank, tearing at the wall and bank -
While blackbirds fly in gusty sighs, the beech tree's arms fills up my eyes - it waves, and flaps, sings *whaa die whee*
Tis time for home, and rest, and tea - while the wind sings on *awharrowhoowharrawhaawhoee!*

Micaela Beckett

ROSES

Roses are so wonderful
Except on days we have to prune
It's then I find them full of spite
With little thorns or little spikes

They tear my flesh, make me bleed
Behind their beauty lies concealed
Little arrows sharp as swords
Is their defence from secateurs?

I always wear my garden gloves
To protect each layer of skin
What does it matter what I do
The thorns can still get in.

Now, I think I have them licked
Well, I don't see any blood
Of course I only fool myself
The thorns are in my gloves

Yet, still I hold them very dear
Especially when their scent is near
The fragrance of the summer rose
Is worth my scars - I can't oppose.

Joan Prentice

FULL MOON OVER CARDIFF BAY

There's a full moon over Cardiff Bay
between depressing, awful autumnal storms.
A cloud shaped like the Hindenburg
caresses the moon and turns orange
so that I reflect on the doomed zeppelin
and how fragile our lives are.

The late November Christmas lights
paint the water with a rainbow of colours
as a chilly unwelcoming wind makes me shiver.
But I like it here without the crowds
lost in my own sea of thoughts
just like the young woman on the edge of tears
as she looks across the tamed waters of Cardiff Bay
with angry storm clouds now wiping the moon away.

Guy Fletcher

MOTHER EARTH

Mother Earth, I hear you groaning
deep down inside.
Your surface is being polluted
every acre far and wide.

Your human tenants love money,
it has become their god.
Greedy, grasping, disloyal
as they pollute your surface, the sod.

When all the fish are gone,
the land is barren and bare,
mankind with his piles of money
will be at last forced to care.

Too late they will see their error
as they slowly start to die.
Their eyes will fill with terror
as on their knees they look at the sky.

In your deep stress Mother Earth
you will laugh and find it funny
as mankind with all his riches
will find that he can't eat money.

Patricia Gray

WILD DAFFODILS

Wild daffodils in forest, field and copse,
Grow with abandon in our village, fair,
A cloth of gold strewn in the spring each year,
Where sunshine flickers through the birch tree tops;
From church to woods we wend our verdant way,
Beside the stream that ripples by the rill,
And gathers speed to Grandpa's water mill,
Secluded home, where corn is ground each day.

A trysting time for villagers nearby,
This festival of flowers our great delight,
Resplendent aisle and pulpit gleaming bright,
A hymn of praise we raise to Heaven on high;
Today we gaze on Kempley's beauteous banks,
For nature's gold, we give our heartfelt thanks.

Norma Rudge

THE RIVER

The river runs deep and still
Bulrushes and reeds line the banks
Coots and moorhens dip in the water
With ducks swimming soundlessly by

Willow branches sweep the edge of the water
Trailing green leaves.
While the water swirls endlessly past . . .
Dark green, hidden depths

Fast-flowing but still and gently swirling on the surface
Deceptively quiet, green, green and deep
No mercy in the deepest depths
Serene and the sound of silence

Deep dark green is the water
Swallows you up if you can't swim
But the stuff of life to fish, herons, ducks and moorhens,
'Tis everything to them, their watery world

Diana Price

THE SPIRIT OF LIFE

As the first snowdrop to open
Or tree buds they form
A chirp from an egg
As a chick struggles forth

The first glimmer of life
A gentle sigh
The twinkle of stars
In the night sky
And glow of a candle in the dark

A softy, downy cheek
A teardrop that slides
In the blink of an eye
The first time a smile
Like a diamond that shines

All our hopes and dreams
For your future little . . . Shannon Marie

Margaret H Mustoe

The Enchanting Cranbourne Chase

A splendour of chalky hills with a summer glory of tall trees
With the unceasing beauty of nature has bestowed
To reveal a splendid display of wild flowers to please
And gently unfolds immutable villages set in a row
Maybe catching a glimpse of the foxgloves in a copse of sand
And along the boundless hedgerows the berries are glowing in the sun
The ever impressive Cranbourne Manor is always looking so grand!
To be able to meander where the peaceful waters flow is fun
In the quiet corners of the fields the cows are munching on the grass
The views all around are spellbinding
As the long road home stretches so long and winding

Sammy Davis

THE ROCKS

The rocks of the
landscape
the coast
and the moors
have been there
forever
for generations
and a score
the rocks lie
in truth
as the people
live and die
they stay as
silent as the
hills, the grass,
and the sky.

Philip Allen

THE DAISIES SUNG

There in a field of many daisies
One stood straight and tall
There stood that beautiful daisy
Pointing its crisp white petals
Into the summer sky
The sun watched over it
While bluebirds sang
A beautiful daisy song

I stood there still
As the sun went in
There was that beautiful daisy
Standing painfully thin
The beauty of that flower
I had never seen before
As I sang along with the bluebirds
To the beautiful daisy song

Victoria Garbutt (12)

Four Seasons

Spring - I am new,
with the potential to
flourish and bloom.

Summer - I am a rose.
Charming all with my beauty.
Radiant in the sunlight.

Autumn - I am the falling leaves.
Passing maturity at sunset,
and going out in a blaze of glory.

Winter - I am cold.
Becoming thin and white,
like the first frost on a barren field.

M M Graham

THE ROSE

A rose for Christmas
A rose for spring
A rose for summer that's the thing
The summer rose that's what you are
To feel you close, deep in my heart
The snows of winter don't fall cold
When it's me, the one you hold
The springtime flowers capture your beauty
Needing you more of all this cutely
My sweet and gorgeous girl of mine
When I'm with you there is no time
To sit and wonder who you are
You hold the beauty of a star
To know you're mine, I can agree
My love for you I must set free
To share your beauty on my own
To call you on the telephone
To hear your sweet and gentle voice
It's hard for me to make my choice
But deep in my heart my love for you
I love my beautiful girl
It's true.

Brian Mcdonagh

SNOWFLAKE

A
frozen,
feathery
drop of water
will, when multiplied
several million-fold,
substantially
transfigure
mighty
Alps.

Norman Bissett

SPRING IN SOMERSET

Rising in light, not in darkness
feels good, gives hopefulness,
spring walks in quietly, slowly,
gathering warmth along the way
signals winter's end, nature's rebirth,
thoughts we cherish for our sanity

A simple treat, blackbirds bathing
frogs, toads, embraced, fertilisation,
green spears piercing the earth
cover it in varied colours
thrill of favoured plants emerging
trees clothing in delicate hues

Sunlight patterned on the walls,
beautiful colours at dawn,
blossom of early cherry trees
garden centres full of buyers
even in a tiny room, flowers will bloom
wonder of a joyful season, a yearly treat.

Monica Redhead

SPRINGTIME IN CAIRO

The appearance of the Bauhinia flowers
are an early sign of spring,
when mustering migrating birds
once more swiftly wing
their instinctive way north
to the land of their birth.

Despite feverish dusty winds
and fierce rain showers
the towering bombax trees
show promising signs of flowers,
each brightly coloured waxy cup
helping to keep our spirits up.

Apricot blossom appears early,
and are cut for decoration,
as the cold winds deter
their ever reaching full fruition,
so these pale blossoms bring
news of the approach of spring.

Marigolds and green ears of barley
are the next to appear
but the arrival of carnations
and irises really brings cheer
to the corner of our street,
putting joy in our hearts and a spring in our feet.

Suzanna Wilson

THE AUTUMN OF LIFE

In the light of the autumn sunshine
I see colours saying their farewell.
A paintbrush is dancing in my mind
Dreaming of the perfect picture
That I wish to paint and leave behind
When the time comes to say my goodbyes.
As the lingering mists clear away,
And rays from a pale October sun
Pick out the highlights and emphasise
The delightful scene on Earth below,
My paintbrush will soon begin to show
The magic powers of this autumn glow.
As I enter the autumn of my years
I'll paint my thanks in glowing colours
I'll show the whole pattern of my life
Unfolding in one brilliant scene.
Vivid tints and new confidence will bring
An autumn that turns once more to spring.

Margaret Nixon

SEASONED GRATITUDE

Big bird circling high
Against the magnet blue sky
Still and humid at ground level
Scents of honeysuckle and rose
Drift upon the near-still air
Mid-summertime for growing thoughts
Everywhere heavy with growth closed in
Playing games as games will be played
Waves of heat and hours that burn with stress
And all about clad in summer dress
Smooth, green, perhaps sand and rock
Or young woman in floral frock
Ah the sweetest scents of meadow hay
Warm, sultry evenings with children at play
Butterflies dance and insects buzz
Dawn chorus of birds a'many calling life
Above mushroomed dew, cool and clear
While the world on a pendulum swings its course
Season to season and back again
My head, my heart, my feelings say 'thank you'.

Clive Cornwall

THE HUNTER

'Did you shoot wild animals
the lion and leopard,
gemsbok and wildebeest?'
was the child's wide-eyed, excited cry.

The blue eyes of the hunter flashed and,
drawing pensively on his pipe
made a quiet reply.
'Some, not many.'

Looking around the plain bare walls,
the disappointed child could not forbear to ask;
'Where are the trophies, heads of bull kudu,
eland and springbok?'

Speaking slowly and with emphasis the
old hunter made this reply.

>'My son, all creatures have the right to life.
>Do not become a thoughtless trophy hunter.
>There is no such thing as hunting for sport.
>You hunt to protect those in need of your protection
>or to put meat on your table.
>*Not* to transfer nature's beauty to your walls.'

Robert Allen

RAINY DAYS

Days of silent, simmering rain
stealthily soaking everything,
of dull, damp, nudging shades of pain,
of murky mists, mysteriously suggesting,
of grim grey rinsing of all frivolity,
of pregnant, still air, barely there.
And treetops static as a picture frame,
their trunks wet, solid as cold stone.
Each leaf heavily dripping, lame,
suspended, until falling alone.
A man's altered step on the street,
bends and bows to Heaven's watery beat,
his hooded voice chastening
with the now sparing birdsong.
And ever quieter growing
with time's downpouring
seeing the sunshine gone,
sensing something's softly over,
simply washed away,
as simple as the rain that day.

Rosalia Campbell Orr

NATURE'S DISAPPEARING

Woodlands, heathlands and hedgerows being lost.
Nature's disappearing to our cost . . .
Folly!
Tread that footpath at your loss;
For the bull in that field 'don't care a toss' . . .

Written 29th April, 1981, of 'Yesterday In Parliament' 8.45 to 9am - just one of the ways that the land-owners keep the public off of 'the public footpaths'

Mary Pauline Winter, nee Coleman

MOTHER EARTH

Breathe into me life
Instil into me honour
Impress upon me honesty
Find within me charity

The fruits of your labour
Will reap you a golden harvest

L E Marchment

THE BLACK HOLE

The hibernating beech stands
Naked before the sombre sky.
Silhouetted trees
Sinewy limbs
Attempt to grasp the heavenly black hole.
The wind whistles an eerie lament
More chilling than the temperature.

Plant life is not dancing
More quaking,
A shuddering with fear.
Bulky cypress hover
Like shadowy villains
Waiting to pounce
On some wandering unsuspecting soul.

Light is internalised
Within this primitive black hole
Of the morning
Only the glint of a street lamp
Somehow defies the darkness
But oh so feebly.

Even the sun
Has been absorbed into the abyss.
As dawn approaches
The earth and the sky
Are black still,
Watchmen of this deep dark winter morn.

Now I know why the solstice
Was such a fearful time for the ancients.

But today
The sun has disappeared from my life
Only darkness remains
Defacing the distant horizon.

John Chambers

WAS THAT A FORECAST?

Today I watched the weatherman say, 'Not a drop of rain
will reach these lovely shores of ours, it's heading out to Spain.'
'Great,' I say, 'the washer's on, I may as well spring clean,
and change the curtains in each room, so everything's pristine.'
First load of washing almost dry, the other load now done,
I'll strip the beds and start them off, make the most of this hot sun,
This task done, one load indoors, the second hanging out,
got stuck into the dusting, till I heard a mighty shout.

The neighbour from across the road was trying to be heard,
'Just thought I'd let you know, it's getting darker over there.'
'Thanks for shouting,' I told her, 'but that will quickly pass,
they say it's off down into Spain, that's today's weather forecast.'
I carried on, the time flew by, the third load must be dry.
I wonder what the time is now, there's a darkness to the sky,
On entering the kitchen, a sight then met my eyes,
no blue was left, just big black clouds, rolling round the skies.

Running down the garden, it was pouring down with rain,
the curtains worse than they went out, need washing once again,
And still I had the bedding to hang out for to dry,
the curtains went back in the wash, no let up from the sky,
It is just a shower that cannot find its way,
needing a little lesson, on the route to southern Spain?
But looking at the sky above, *no chance,* my brain did say,
this is not a shower, it's in now for the day.

I wish I had an aeroplane, I'd fly across the land and find
the place where that man lives, then with the washing in my hand,
Say, 'Due to your bad forecast, I stripped all of the beds,
the curtains and a full day's wash,' then tip it on his head,
'Now you can wash this lot again, and get all of it dry,
for I believed you when you said no cloud would mar the sky,
When that's all done, you bring them back, am I making myself plain?
Don't look at me to help you, get you own transport to Spain.'

Kathleen Townsley

SUBMISSIONS INVITED
SOMETHING FOR EVERYONE

POETRY NOW 2003 - Any subject, any style, any time.

WOMENSWORDS 2003 - Strictly women, have your say the female way!

STRONGWORDS 2003 - Warning! Opinionated and have strong views. (Not for the faint-hearted)

All poems no longer than 30 lines.
Always welcome! No fee!
Cash Prizes to be won!

Mark your envelope (eg *Poetry Now*) **2003**
Send to:
Forward Press Ltd
Remus House, Coltsfoot Drive,
Peterborough, PE2 9JX

**OVER £10,000 POETRY PRIZES
TO BE WON!**

Judging will take place in October 2003